DISCOVERING POMPEII

BOOK I: DISCOVERING ANCIENT SITES

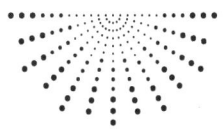

NATASHA SHELDON

STRIGIDAE PRESS

Copyright © 2018 by Natasha Sheldon

All rights reserved.

No part of this book may be reproduced in any form or by any electronic or mechanical means, including information storage and retrieval systems, without written permission from the author, except for the use of brief quotations in a book review.

Cover Design: Jack Clements

*To Neil for your patience and support.
And for Marcus, who is looking forward to exploring "The Big Volcano'
and its "Broken City" for the first time, very soon.*

ACKNOWLEDGMENTS

The author would like to thank Peter Clements and Jeffrey Jacobson for their kind permission to use plans and images of reconstructions.

And, last but by no means, least, a massive 'Thank You' to Jack Clements for the wonderful cover.

CONTENTS

Foreword — xi
Introduction — xv

Part I
CIVIC POMPEII

1. The Making of a Town — 3
2. Early Pompeii — 6
3. A Crossroad of Cultures — 10
4. Hellenization — 16
5. The Monumental Gateway — 20
6. Introduction to the Forum — 24
7. Governing Pompeii — 30
8. The Roman Conquest — 34
9. Cultural Change — 38
10. The Capitolium — 44
11. New Civic Amenities — 47
12. Slaves and Civic Religion — 53
13. Pompeii's Pardon — 57
14. The Imperial Cult — 61
15. Women in Pompeii — 65
16. The Rise of the Mystery Cult — 71

Part II
DAILY LIFE IN POMPEII

17. The Via dell'Abbondanza — 77
18. Public Bathing — 83
19. Pompeii's Water Supply — 87
20. The State of the Streets — 90
21. Trade and Industry — 94
22. Popular Religion — 99
23. Innovative Housing — 104
24. Interior Design — 109
25. Eat, Drink and be Merry — 114

26. Ordinary Apartments	118
27. Daily Bread	121
28. The Pompeian Familia	126
29. Pompeii's Gardens	132
30. Graffiti and Politics	136
31. Gladiators	141
32. A Country Villa in the Town	145
33. Small Gardens	149
34. A High Class Leisure Centre	153
35. Vintage Pompeii	156
36. Spectacula	160

Part III
POMPEII'S LAST DAYS

37. Introduction	169
38. Dating the Eruption	172
39. Sign and Portents	176
40. Vesuvius Awakes	181
41. The Umbrella Pine	183
42. A Lethal Rainfall	186
43. Hiding Treasure	189
44. Hope Fades	193
45. The Violence Escalates	198
46. No Refuge	200
47. Midnight Terrors	203
48. The Early Hours of the Morning	206
49. The Third Surge Part I	212
50. The Third Surge Part II.	217
51. The Great Leveller	222
52. The Fourth Surge	226
53. The Fourth Surge, Part II	230
54. The Fifth Surge	233
55. The Fifth Surge Part II	236
56. The End of Pompeii	240
57. The Nucerian Gate	248
Before You Go…	253

Picture Credits	255
Bibliography	263
Footnotes	267
About the Author	273
Also by Natasha Sheldon	275

FOREWORD

INTRODUCTION TO THE SECOND EDITION.

Pompeii is a 'must see' sight for many of Campania's tourists. For many, its tragic and dramatic end, coupled with the chance to explore the streets and buildings of an ancient city is a lure too strong to resist.

It is possible to cover most of Pompeii in a day-if you want to skimp. During that day, you can wander about its streets, lingering at buildings that capture your imagination. However, you won't learn about the history of the city - its story, if you will. Nor will you necessarily understand what part the building or street you find yourself in plays in that story.

To best discover Pompeii, you need a guide. One that gives you a route to follow and explains the archaeology you encounter. This book aims to do just that - but with a twist. For it's tours don't just introduce you to the buildings (although they do that too). Instead, they use the physical remains of Pompeii to reveal three different strands of Pompeii's history. **Civic Pompeii** explores Pompeii from its Oscan beginnings to its Roman end by analysing the areas around the Triangular and Main *fora*. **A Walk Down the Via dell' Abbondanza**, focuses on one of Pompeii's

FOREWORD

major thoroughfares to impart a general feel of the day-to-day life of the town- and everyday Roman life in general. Finally, **Pompeii's Last Days** takes the visitor through the streets of Pompeii on a point-by-point tour of each of the stages of the eruption of Vesuvius in 79AD- and how the people of Pompeii experienced it.

~

Pliny the Younger's account of the eruption of Vesuvius was the first ancient text I read at the age of ten. Pliny's vivid recollections captured me immediately and started an obsession with Pompeii, Herculaneum and the other doomed towns of the region that lasts to this day. Since then, I have visited Pompeii five times. I have explored its streets and buildings, studied them and interviewed experts on the conservation of the town, the body casts of its population and the effects of the eruption.

This second edition of *Discovering Pompeii* is the final stage in the evolution of a project that I have been working on since 2011. *Discovering Pompeii* began life as an iPhone walking tour concentrating on the Via dell Abbondanza. Eventually, it became three separate eBooks. Finally, I compiled it into one volume of all three tours. So what is different in this final incarnation?

Well, the themed tours remain the same but the maps and illustrations are fewer. However, the crucial difference is in the detail I give to accompany the tours. The initial versions concentrated on the story - with little emphasis on the archaeology/layout of the individual buildings outside of the scope of the particular theme. This new version of *Discovering Pompeii* provides an overview of some of the buildings as well as background snippets to explain historical terminology and give a little more context. The book can be used as a tour guide around Pompeii, but also functions equally as well as a general historical guide that sets Pompeii in the wider context of Roman history.

However you use the book, I hope it achieves it aims: to inform, to entertain and to make you want to know more about this unique archaeological site.

Natasha Sheldon
2018

INTRODUCTION

GENERAL INFORMATION

How to Reach Pompeii.

The easiest way to reach Pompeii is by the **Circumvesuviana train service**. The closest stop for the main entrance at Porta Marina and Piazza Esedra is the **Pompeii Villa dei Mystery** stop. To reach here, take the Napoli-Sorrento line. Alternatively, you can head for the **Piazza Anfiteatro Entrance** by taking the Napoli-Poggiomarino line. Alight at the Pompeii Santuario stop if this is the entrance you opt for.

Train times and further information can be found at:

http://www.sitabus.it/en/circumvesuviana-timetables-and-rates/

Pompeii can also be reached by **SITA bus** that runs between Naples and Salerno.

By Car: Take the A3 Naples-Salerno Motorway and exit at 'Pompeii West.'

INTRODUCTION

Opening Times:

1 April-31 October: 8.30am-7.30pm.

1 November-31 March: 8.30am-5pm. (Last ticket sales are at 3.30pm)

∼

Tickets

Single Tickets, valid for a one-day visit of the site are available at both entrances. They cost 13 euros full price or 7 euros if you have a concession. Under 18s can enter for free and if you are between 18-24, you can get a concessionary ticket from the European Union. Present a passport, driving license or some other ID at the point of sales to qualify.

On the first Sunday of each month, entrance to the site is free for all.

(This information is valid at the time of publication)

∼

Site Amenities.

Toilets, refreshments, and left luggage points can all be found close to the entrances at the Piazza Esedra and Piazza Anfiteatro. This is useful if you arrive with baggage, as this is not allowed inside Pompeii.

About the site itself, you will find, toilets, refreshment areas and a first aid point to the north of the forum on the Via degli Augustali and the Via del Foro.

INTRODUCTION

For further information, see:
http://www.pompeiisites.org/Sezione.jsp?titolo=TICKETS+AND+INFO&idSezione=6786

Advisements

• Good shoes for walking on uneven surfaces
• Certain areas of the site are unsuitable for wheelchairs or pushchairs because of the uneven nature of Pompeii's streets
• Water, a hat or sunshade in summer.
• September/October is a good time to visit, as you can avoid the worst of the crowds and the summer heat- and also the worst of the winter weather.

Warnings

Be careful when travelling to Pompeii and around the site itself. The Bay of Naples area is notorious for its very skilled pickpockets and petty criminals. Avoid wearing visible jewellery and keep valuables and money out of sight.

If you are a victim of crime, a police station can be found at the Piazza Esedra, to the right of the Porto Marina entrance to the site.

Please be aware that maintenance and conservation work is ongoing at Pompeii. This may mean that certain areas of the site mentioned in this guide may be closed to the public at times.

INTRODUCTION

PART I
CIVIC POMPEII

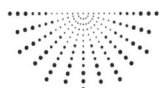

TEMPLES, FORA AND THE MAKING OF A CITY

1
THE MAKING OF A TOWN

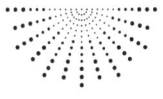

INTRODUCTION

POMPEII WAS MORE THAN JUST A ROMAN TOWN. IT WAS FOUNDED BY the Oscan tribes that were the early inhabitants of Campania. However, Pompeii was also inhabited and influenced by other peoples and cultures. The Etruscans, Samnites, Northern Italic tribes and the Greeks that settled on the southern coast of Italy all left their mark on the town.

With time, Pompeii rose to become a wealthy and influential Italic town. First, she was a friend to Rome, then a rebel. Finally, Pompeii's former ally made her a Roman colony.

Pompeii's varied history can be read in her public buildings: her temples, administrative buildings — even the bathhouses and leisure areas. These buildings concentrate in two areas: the triangular forum and the main forum. These are the sacred and secular centres of Pompeii, and the story of their beginnings and evolution is also the story of Pompeii's foundation and growth.

Figure 1: Tour Route for 'Civic Pompeii'

DISCOVERING POMPEII

Key

- A. The Triangular Forum
- B. The Doric Temple
- C. The Quadroporticus
- D. The Monumental Gateway
- E. Intersection
- F. The Basilica
- G. The Temple of Venus
- H. The Temple of Apollo
- I. The Capitolium
- J. The Forum Baths
- K. The Temple of Augustan Fortune
- L. The Augustan Forum
- M. The Temple to the Lares and the Temple of Vespasian
- N. The Eumachia Building
- O. The Temple of Isis
- A. The Triangular Forum

2
EARLY POMPEII

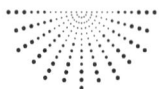

THE TRIANGULAR FORUM

The land that became the city of Pompeii was first settled in prehistory. The earliest object discovered on the site was a stone axe from the **Chalcolithic era**. Other pottery fragments from Region V of the site suggest settlement during the Bronze Age.[1]

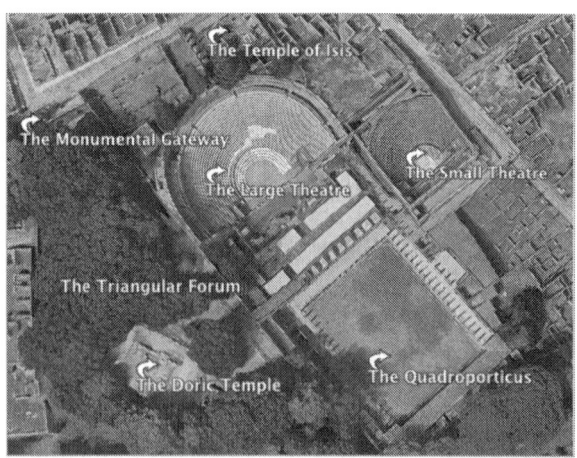

Figure 2: Plan of the Triangular Forum

DISCOVERING POMPEII

The fledgling settlement began as little more than a cluster of farmsteads. But by the sixth century BC, it began to display some of the attributes of a town. We know from terracotta decoration and votive deposits from the sanctuary of Apollo that a temple was established in the area of the main forum during this early period, making it one of Pompeii's earliest civic buildings[2].

The Chalcolithic Period

The Chalcolithic period occurred between the Neolithic and Bronze Age (approx 4500-3000 BC in Europe). It is the era marked by the transition from stone to metal tools and is sometimes known as the copper age.

Pompeii's first city wall, the *pappamonte tufa*[3], was erected during this era.

However, most of the land inside that wall was still farmland and vineyards. But in the southwest corner of the town, a web of irregular streets was growing up beneath the northern and western slopes of an isolated triangular spur of lava that rose above the land around it.

The final evidence for early Pompeii can be found here, on that triangular spur, in the Triangular Forum. Postholes have been found here dating to 600BC. However, they did not belong to houses. For the singular nature of the lava spur made it a natural sacred spot. The early inhabitants of Pompeii left votive deposits of ceramics and terracotta pottery here and established the town's other early sanctuary, the Doric Temple.

~

Did You Know?....

Pompeii was built on a lava platform formed by an earlier eruption of Vesuvius. This plateau was the only defensible site in the otherwise flat marshland of the River Sarno — the perfect site for a town!

~

It was around the base of the Triangular Forum that the early inhabitants of Pompeii built the first streets. This area is known as the *Alstadt*[4].

Who were the people who founded these sanctuaries? Both Strabo[5] and Pliny the Elder[6] describe the earliest inhabitants of Pompeii as Oscan. But even at the beginning of its life, Pompeii was a crossroads of cultures.

~

Did You Know?.....

Only 2% of Pompeii has been excavated below the 79AD level of activity.

~

The next stopping point, the Doric Temple, lies just ahead, to the right.

DISCOVERING POMPEII

3
A CROSSROAD OF CULTURES

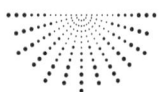

THE DORIC TEMPLE

THE OSCANS WERE THE ORIGINAL PREHISTORIC INHABITANTS OF Campania, with their territory initially stretching across southern Italy. However, by the sixth century BC, this territory diminished as the Oscans became caught between the southern advance of the Etruscans and the Greeks who had settled the Campanian coastline two centuries before.

Figure 3: Recreation of how the Doric Temple would have looked viewed from the South

DISCOVERING POMPEII

The so-called Doric Temple was built during this period to celebrate the sacred nature of the Triangular Forum. As figure 3 shows, it dominated the landscape of Pompeii and was visible even from outside the city walls. Although the Oscans initially constructed the temple, its architecture and chosen gods show Greek and Etruscan influences at work.

~

Did You Know?....

Oscan continued to be spoken in and around Pompeii throughout its history.

~

The layout of Greek and Etruscan temples were different to each other. Greek temples consisted of a podium surrounded by steps. The central *cella*, which housed the cult statue, was surrounded by a single or double collonaded peristyle. The columns on the long side of this peristyle were double plus one those of the width. Finally, at the back of the temple was a false porch or *opisthodomos* that often acted as the temple treasury.

~

The Greeks and Early Pompeii.

In approximately 650BC, Greek city-states began planting colonies around the Bay of Naples, at Cumae and Naples. Eventually,

Greek influence spread to Pompeii. Evidence of this early Hellenisation includes mason marks carved in Greek letters on the city wall.

Etruscan temples only had columns and steps at the front. The *cella* also divided into three. Unlike Greek temples, whose pediments were decorated with sculptures, Etruscan temples had statues on the roof.

The Etruscans

An indigenous Italic people from northern Italy, the Etruscans spread their culture further south into Campania during the eighth century BC. While Capua became one of their major towns in the region, Etruscan influence also reached Pompeii.

Etruscan Bucchero pottery, a form of black ceramic drinking vessel, has been found around the Temple of Apollo. This probably reached Pompeii via trade.

Pompeii's Doric Temple combined Etruscan terracotta decorations with the archaic Greek Doric columns that give the temple its name. The arrangement of these columns — seven on the short sides and eleven on the long sides — meant that they could not have framed one central cult statue in the *cella*. Instead, this odd arrangement suggests two statues were framed, indicating the Doric Temple was dedicated to two deities. Evidence from the remains of the sculpted metopes that ran around the temple's roof suggests one of these gods was the Etruscan goddess Minerva. The other could have been the Greek hero Herakles or Hercules as he was known in Latin.

Figure 4: Hercules fighting Geryon (on the far right). Eruption lies wounded at the hero's feet while Athena (to the left) overlooks the scene.

A terracotta **antefix** of the hero remains from this early temple. Hercules was closely linked to the foundation of Pompeii and remained a favourite mythological figure throughout the town's history.

Antefix:

"an upright ornament at the eaves of a tiled roof, to conceal the foot of a row of convex tiles that cover the joints of the flat tiles"[1]

According to legend, Hercules passed through Pompeii after defeating Geryon, driving the monster's cattle as he progressed. This procession or *'pompe'* may have given Pompeii its name if the ancient writer Isidore[1] is to be believed.

Did You Know?....

Pompeii's name could also have derived from the Italic word for five — 'pompe'. This could be a reference to the five settlements that amalgamated to form the original town.

The picture on the previous page shows Athena watching over Hercules. The goddess was his patron and the Greek equivalent of Minerva. Whether the Greeks or Etruscans ever ruled early Pompeii is debatable. But their two cultures married harmoniously in the Doric temple.

Figure 5: Bas-relief of Minerva or Menerva, the Italian goddess of handicrafts

However, this harmonious blending of Greek and Etruscan cultures in the Doric temple did not reflect reality. By the fifth century, the two cultures were clashing in southern Italy. In 474BC, at the Battle of Cumae, the Greeks defeated the Etruscans with the help of their Sicilian allies. The Greeks were now the dominant power in the Bay of Naples. That dominance began to show itself in Pompeii.

This is demonstrated at the next stopping point. Leave the Doric temple behind you now and move forward, turning left at the staircase leading to the palestra and the large theatre.

4
HELLENIZATION

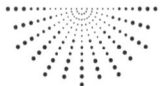

THE QUADROPORTICUS

Figure 6: The Quadroporticus

BY THE EARLY FIFTH CENTURY BC, MILITARY DEFEATS HAD BROKEN the Greek and Etruscan dominance of Campania. Pompeii may even have been briefly abandoned because of the conflict in the region. But by the mid-fifth century, the town was on the up again.

The Samnites, an Oscan-speaking tribe from the central-southern Apennines, had filled the power vacuum. Pompeii became part of the Samnite Confederacy, a conglomerate of local towns that included Herculaneum, Nuceria, Surrentum and Stabiae.

The Samnites and the Samnite Confederacy

The Samnites were a warlike people. They were divided into four tribal states: the Caraceni, the Caudini, the Hirpini and the Pentri. Together, these tribes formed the Samnite Confederacy and were bound to support each other in war.

The Samnites became the enemies of Rome in the third and fourth centuries BC. In all, three wars were fought between the two peoples — conflicts that became known as the Samnite Wars. These wars ended with the total subjugation of the Samnite nation by Rome.

However, by the third century BC, the Samnites were also declining, while Rome's fortunes were now in the ascendant. So the Pompeians cannily allied with the new power as they needed to protect their interests. Boom time had come to the town as Pompeii became wealthy from trading olive oil and wine with the East.

Despite this instinct for self-preservation, Pompeii stood by its new ally throughout the Punic Wars against Carthage. Unlike many other Italian cities, Pompeii survived the wars unscathed and continued to thrive.

However, when it came to inspiration for enhancing its

appearance, Pompeii looked to Greece. Hellenisation was the process whereby Greek ideas and styles spread to other cultures. By the second century AD, Greek culture was the height of fashion in Campania and any city wanting to acquire status was wise to emulate it. The result was a series of Hellenistic cultural imports into Pompeii. The **Large Theatre** was one of the first.

The Large Theatre was built in the second century BC. It took a typical Greek form. A seating area designed to accommodate up to 5000 spectators — known as the *Cavea* — was built into the natural slope of the Triangular Forum. Roman theatres had wide, semi-circular stages. However, Vitruvius described Greek stages as circular[1]. The stage of the Large Theatre at Pompeii conformed to the Greek style. It was also one metre lower than in a Roman theatre.

Figure 7: Computer Reconstruction of the Hellenistic theatre and Triangular Forum

The Large Theatre hosted the Greek plays and musical entertainments that the people of Pompeii were beginning to enjoy so much. However, the arts were not the only Greek fashions that Pompeians adopted.

The Greeks were also known as the *'Men of the gymnasium'*[2.] Greek gyms were not just places to exercise; they were places to celebrate the excellence of both body and mind. Exercise took place in a central courtyard. Athletes could also relax in the shade of the surrounding colonnades and side rooms and discuss philosophy and the arts.

The area behind the Large Theatre in Pompeii fits the ground plan of a Greek gymnasium perfectly. Known as the **Quadroporticus**, it was erected by the *duovir* Vibius Vinicius with money left by Vibius Adiranus for the good of Pompeii's youth[3]. A staircase connected the quadroporticus to the rest of the Triangular Forum. At the top of this staircase, a miniature athletics stadium dating from the same period ran along the forum's edge.

∼

Who Ruled Pompeii?

Oscan Inscriptions show that a popular assembly overseen by a council ruled early Pompeii.

In some respects, this government was very similar to that of the Romans, with the same kinds of civic officials and duties.

Aediles were in charge of Pompeii's roads, Quaestors the town's finances and magistrates sponsored public buildings as a means of winning popular support.

∼

Pompeii also used Greek architectural styles to enhance its existing civic structures. Return to the Triangular Forum and exit onto the Via del Tempio d"Iside for the next stopping point, the Monumental Gateway.

5
THE MONUMENTAL GATEWAY

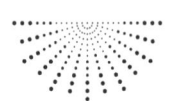

Figure 8: The Remains of the Monumental Gateway

AS WELL AS BUILDING NEW HELLENISTIC LEISURE FACILITIES, wealthy Pompeians started to invest in renovating the Triangular Forum. This was not just for Pompeii's benefit but also to help the new elite impress the citizen body — especially at election time.

Prominent Pompeii Families

Throughout Pompeii's history, a number of monied aristocratic families dominated Pompeii's civic landscape. These families, whose wealth lay invested in land and agriculture, helped monumentalise the city so they could gain political influence. Amongst them were the Popidii, with Vibius Popidius dedicating several monuments in his name, including the Nolan Gate. The Holconii were also another landed aristocratic family who made a massive impact in the Augustan period with projects such as their renovation of the Large Theatre.

The Doric Temple was rebuilt and a colonnade added to the edge of the forum itself, helping define its shape. The final embellishment was a new **monumental gateway** at the entrance of the forum. This gateway announced the Triangular Forum as the sacred and cultural centre of Pompeii.

Figure 9: Computer Reconstruction of the Monumental gateway

As you can see from the picture, the gateway consisted of six Ionic columns. Behind the columns were the entrances to the forum. The middle entrance was for everyday use, guiding people towards the theatre and gym. The eastern entrance was used infrequently. This was the ceremonial entrance to the forum, where sacred processions would pass to and from the Doric Temple.

Marcus Holconius Rufus

Marcus Holconius Rufus was probably the most successful member of the Holconii family during the Augustan period, using civic beneficence to ensure he enjoyed a long and prominent public life. One of his major projects was the renovation of the large theatre. The town council was so grateful for his contribution that they awarded Holconius a dedicated permanent seat, which gave him the best views of the stage. It came complete with his name in lavish bronze letters.

Holconius's civic building schemes ensured he enjoyed an unprecedented number of political appointments over his career. He was elected chief magistrate or quinquennalis at least once and was appointed duumvir no less than five times. However, Holconius did not just court success in Pompeii. One of his less popular local building schemes was the renovation of the temple of Apollo. One of the sanctuary's new walls obscured the light to local houses, obliging Holconius to pay the householders compensation. Alienating potential voters was hardly a good move for a canny politician. However, Apollo was the patron god of the Emperor Augustus. Holconius must have judged that a little local disgruntlement was worthwhile if he managed to attract the attention of the Emperor himself.

The ploy must have worked because Holconius was one of the few members of the local Pompeian elite to be appointed as Pompeii's patron. A patron was supposed to represent his town's interests in Rome — not something that could be undertaken if the individual did not have influence. Clearly, Marcus Holconius Rufus performed this role well, for the town council held him in such high regard that it awarded him a statue at the next stopping point at the intersection between the Via Stabiana and the Via dell' Abbondanza.

∼

6
INTRODUCTION TO THE FORUM

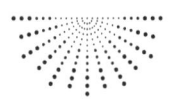

THE INTERSECTION BETWEEN THE VIA DELL ABBONDANZA AND VIA DEL TEATRI

Figure 10: Intersection between the Via del Teatri and the Via dell'Abbondanza.

THE MONUMENTAL GATEWAY WAS DESIGNED AS A FEATURE TO BE viewed from a distance. When observed from this intersection with the Via dell'Abbondanza and the Via del Teatri, the gateway drew the eye, reminding the viewer of the importance of the area it marked1. For the intersection was not simply a crossroads; it also acted as a link between the sacred and the secular civic areas of Pompeii.

DISCOVERING POMPEII

The bollards surrounding the intersection would have stopped or slowed the flow of traffic, causing it to pause at the intersection. If the onlooker glanced ahead, their eye was drawn to the Monumental Gateway. However, if they looked right, they could see one of the entrances to Pompeii's main forum.

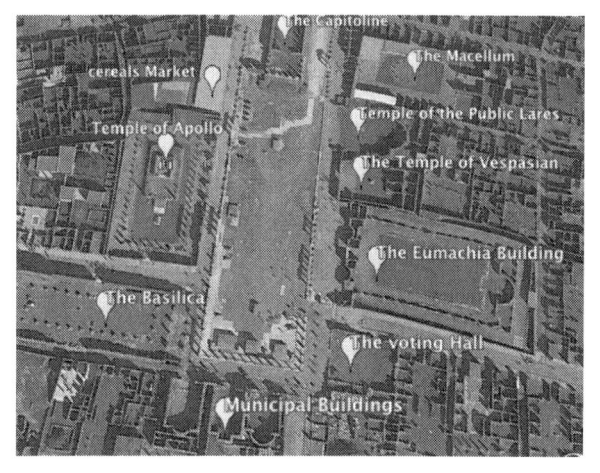

Figure 11: Overview of the main forum

Before the second century BC, the main forum as a monumental civic centre did not really exist. It was simply an irregularly shaped open space, accessible from the many streets which converged upon it. Edged with houses and shops on its east side, the Sanctuary of Apollo dominated the space to the west.

The forum at this time was essentially an open market area. Its proximity to the coast and the River Sarno — both major sources of trade — made it a natural commercial centre.

"Nola, Nuceria and Adhere have as their port Pompeii on the River Sarno, which transports goods in both directions."

(Strabo, Geography 5.4.8)

~

In the Second Century BC, this began to change. The Triangular Forum may have been Pompeii's sacred and cultural centre, but it was too limited in space and too peripheral to accommodate the range of buildings needed to administrate the growing town.

So, this market area began to develop into a centre of administration and government. Pompeii's main forum began to evolve.

~

Trade in Pompeii

Trade in Pompeii took many forms. The city was a centre of manufacturing, famous for its garum or fish sauce, as well as wine and local fruit. However, Pompeii was also a major importer of foreign wine and luxury goods such as silks, perfumes, spices, pottery and glass from Egypt and the East. These goods were sold at local markets or **nundinae** *whose schedules were advertised on the walls of buildings around the town.*

The forum was the place for these business transactions to take place — under the careful eye of town officials. One of the relics of this official monitoring in the forum is a marble "weights and measures' table-a **Mensa Ponderaria**. *The Mensa Ponderaria was established during Pompeii's Samnite period and later amended by the Romans. It consisted* *of a number of circular cavities cut into a table, used to measure goods for trade.*

~

Garum

Made from rotted, fermented fish guts, garum was a type of fish sauce that the Romans loved to use as a condiment. Pompeii was famed for the quality of its garum, which was manufactured close to the River Sarno. Here, local producers were right next to its primary ingredients: fish and salt. They were also far enough away from the rest of the town to spare people the smell of the garum making process!

The fish guts were steeped in salt in large terracotta pots before being covered and left to mature. Once ready, the garum was sold in long, one-handled jugs called Urcei.

There were various grades of garum. **Liquamen** *was the best quality sauce, made from the first sieving. The highest-grade liquamen was known as* **Haimation** *and made from tuna rather than the standard mackerel. The remains of the garum making process were sold as a poor quality product called* **Hallex***.*

~

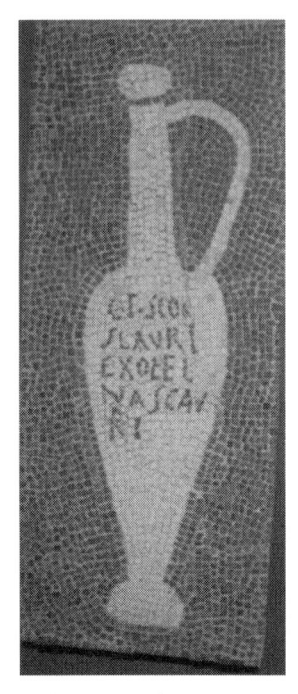

Figure 12: Mosaic of Garum Amphorae of Aulus Umbricius Scarus

Aulus Umbricius Scarus

In Pompeii, the pre-eminent producer of garum was Aulus Umbricius Scarus. Over 50 containers bearing Scarus's name have been found around Pompeii and its environs. Around 30% of the sauce containers in Campania also came from Scarus's workshops, which gives some idea of the exact scale of his business.

Scarus made a fortune from his business, as his house attested. This lies to the west of Pompeii at VII, 16.15, beyond the scope of this tour. Overlooking the sea, the house was three stories high. Scarus's home was opulent and equipped with a collonaded garden, its own bath suite and no less than three atria. Unlike the homes of some of Pompeii's citizens, *archaeologists had no trouble identifying its owner. For decorating the floor around the impluvium in one of the atria was a mosaic adorned with four larger than life black and white urcei, each inscribed with Scarus's name and advertising the excellence of his garum.*

Each mosaic urcei boasted of the merits of a particular brand of Scarus's fish sauce, whether it was high or low grade. "The flower of Scarus's mackerel garum from the factory of Scarus," announced the lettering next to the urcei relating to Scarus's liquamen. Some local aristocrats may have found this blatant advertising crass. Crass or not, it made good sense. After all, the atrium was where Scarus met his business associates. He probably thought it was as well to let his décor do some of the talking for him.

∽

Turn right at the intersection and walk down the Via dell' Abbondanza. Turn left onto the southernmost side of the main forum. One of these new civic buildings was the basilica, numbered VIII.I.2 on Pompeii's plan.

∽

7
GOVERNING POMPEII

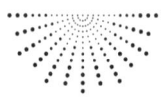

THE BASILICA

Figure 13: The Remains of the Basilica

BASILICAS BEGAN LIFE IN GREECE AS AUDIENCE CHAMBERS FOR Hellenistic kings. Later, they spread to other Greek and Roman cities as administration centres. Eventually, their design was adopted by early Christian churches.

Pompeii's basilica is one of the earliest Italian examples. Situated at the southwest end of the forum, it dates to 78BC. We know this because a Gaius Pumidius Dipilus scrawled his name on the plaster inside the building and added reference points for the date: namely the consuls in Rome at the time.1

Figure 14: Reconstruction of the Exterior of the Basilica

Dipilus's Inscription on the Basilica.

"C(aius) Pumidius Dipilus heic fuit a(nte) d(iem) V nonas Octobreis M(arco) Lepid(o), Q(uinto) Catul(o) co(nsulibus"

This roughly translates as "Gaius Pumidius Dipilus was here five days before the nones of October when Marcus Lepidus and Quintus Catullus were Consuls in Rome during the year 78BC."[2]

∽

Figure 15: Aerial overview of the Basilica. A. Main Entrance, B. Side Aisle 1, C. Side Aisle 2, D. Portico, E. Nave. F. Tribunal, G.Secondary Entrance.

The pictures and plan give some indication of the Basilica's appearance — inside and out. It was built to provide Pompeians with somewhere to conduct legal proceedings and business transactions. Covering an area of 1480 metres squared, its main entrance was on its short side facing the forum, with two smaller entrances off the Porta Marina.

The basilica's interior hall was two stories high and flanked by a four-sided portico of twenty-eight 11-metre-high Ionic columns. This hall divided into a nave and two side aisles. The tribunal was at the back of the central nave, a raised platform where the city officials could address large gatherings. This tribunal was reached by a ladder that could be pulled up if things became rowdy, thus protecting officials from the crowd.

Along with the three buildings to its right: the *Curia*, the meeting place of the town council, the *Tabularium* or town archive and the office of the duumvirs and aediles, the basilica was central to Pompeii's governance and symbolic of the town's self-autonomy.

∼

This independent identity was not to last. Pompeii was about to turn against its old ally, Rome. It was a move that had disastrous consequences for the city. The Temple of Venus, our next stopping point, can be found at VIII.1.3, left of the Basilica and further down the Via Marina. It was a symbol of the newly conquered Pompeii's loss of self-autonomy.

∼

8
THE ROMAN CONQUEST

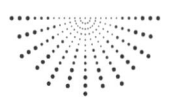

THE TEMPLE OF VENUS

Figure 16: Layout of the Temple of Venus. A. Main Entrance. B. Secondary Entrance. C. Cella, D. Double Colonnade. E. Altar.

POMPEII AND THE OTHER ITALIAN ALLIES WANTED TO ENJOY ALL THE benefits of Roman citizenship as a reward for their long years of support. Rome refused them. The Social War was the result and Pompeii took a leading role. In 89BC, the forces of dictator Sulla besieged Pompeii and starved the town into submission.

The Social Wars 91-89BC

By the second century BC, Rome had dominated the other Italic states. So, she established a series of alliances and treaties designed to guarantee a harmonious and supportive co-existence between all parties.

However, Rome's allies were not happy. Their alliances with the city placed them under certain obligations, for instance, supplying Rome with extra troops during the Punic Wars. The allies felt, however, that Rome was taking them for granted. They believed that states in the Etruscan heartlands were more favourably treated as Rome had awarded them citizen status. In contrast, the other Italic states had surrendered their self-autonomy for little recompense.

So, Rome's former Italic allies went to war — to gain Roman citizenship rather than their lost independence.

Ironically, Pompeii received the citizenship it craved after its defeat — but at a cost. Pompeii's leading citizens had to pay fines in land and money that ruined many of them. But worse still, the city lost its independence. In 80BC, around 2000 Sullan veterans and their families settled in the town. Pompeii became a Roman colony that was renamed *Colonia Veneria Cornella Pompeianorum.*

Figure 17: Venus watching over Aeneas

Venus was the patron goddess of Sulla. She was also the mother of the Trojan hero Aeneas from whom the Romans claimed descent. The inclusion of her name in Pompeii's new title commemorated the support the Romans believed the goddess gave them. For that reason, the Romans dedicated a new temple to Venus close to the forum.

The Temple of Venus (VIII.I.3) may have been built over a temple dedicated to the Samnite love goddess, Mephitis or one belonging to a fertility cult similar to that of Magna Mater-the Great Mother[1]. Several houses were also demolished to accommodate the new temple, which now covered an area of 300 metres square — over 3000 square feet. Little of the temple remains today. However, it is clear from the remaining fragments that the temple's *cella* floor consisted of a central panel of polychrome marble, surrounded by a border of white mosaic.

Rome's choice of location for its new temple was not simply to associate it with Pompeii's existing goddess of love. The Temple of Venus's position was also strategic. The new temple dominated Pompeii's skyline. It was this new Roman temple rather than the old Doric temple in the Triangular Forum that people first glimpsed when approaching Pompeii. Rome was using Venus as a symbol of her dominance.

∾

The Romans also expressed their dominance in other ways. On the Via Marina, turn towards the forum again and head for the Temple of Apollo at VII.7.32 on the left.

∾

9
CULTURAL CHANGE

THE TEMPLE OF APOLLO

Figure 18: Reconstruction of the Temple of Apollo

THE ROMANS IMPOSED THEIR CULTURE AS WELL AS THEIR PHYSICAL presence on Pompeii. The town government was reorganised to mirror that of Rome and Pompeii was split into wards or *vici*, the borders of which were marked with altars to the local Lares — the guardian spirits that Romans believed protected a marked area of land.

The Political Hierarchy of Pompeii

The Populus was composed of all free, male citizens of good character and property. This group of Pompeians were eligible to vote for Pompeii's town officials. During the Roman era, these officials consisted of:

Duoviri/Duumvir or "The Two Men". These were the two chief magistrates of Pompeii who presided over meetings and tribunals. Their role was very similar to that of Consuls in Rome.

Aedilis. Subordinate to the duoviri, the aedilis were the civic magistrates responsible for urban maintenance and entertainment.

Ordo Decurionum. The 100 town magistrates, composed of ex duoviri. All derived from Pompeii's elite.

∼

The most striking change was to the official language of Pompeii. There were three main groups of Italic language: Umbrian, Latin and Oscan. Throughout its history, Pompeii had remained Oscan-speaking. All written records, from official inscriptions to casual graffiti, were in the language of the city's founders. This now changed. Latin, the language of Rome, became the primary language of Pompeii.

Figure 19: Layout of the Temple of Apollo. A. Cella, B. podium, C. Altar, D. Colonnaded Court, E. Entrances.

The Colour of the Temple of Apollo.

Greek and Roman Classical temples were not the plain white edifices we see today; instead, they were brightly painted.

The temple of Apollo was painted yellow, with the capitals of its columns highlighted with blue and red.

Inscriptions on all new buildings built after the conquest, such as the amphitheatre and the odeon in the Triangular Forum, were now in Latin. Latin translations were also added to pre-existing civic monuments.

The Sanctuary of Apollo was, alongside the Doric temple, Pompeii's most ancient sanctuary site. It may originally have been dedicated to a female goddess such as Ceres but became associated with Apollo as the god's cult spread from nearby Cumae.

The sanctuary was constructed from grey Nucerian tufa and consisted of a central temple surrounded by a peristyle of nine columns on its north and south side and 17 columns to the East and west. A statue of the god Apollo helped identify the sanctuary to excavators — along with his name, inscribed into the precinct pavement.

Unlike the Doric Temple, the Sanctuary of Apollo was still a key civic feature by the time of the Roman conquest. But modifications made to the sanctuary after the Romans took over show how the sanctuary was displaced in the civic hierarchy.

The Sanctuary of Apollo had undergone major renovations just before the Social War and so was in a good state of repair by the time Pompeii became a Roman colony. The extent of its *temenos* or sacred space had shrunk during the second-century modifications to the forum. So, to emphasise the sanctuary's continual importance, the Pompeians connected the sanctuary to the forum with eleven new entrances.

Sulla's Roman colonists blocked these new entrances off to show the sanctuary's diminished importance in the new Pompeii. The temple's existing altar was also unnecessarily replaced with a new one. The donors of this superfluous gift ensured that their names were clearly visible upon it. These donors, Marcus Porcius, Lucius Sextilius and Gaius Cornelius, were all Romans — and they inscribed their dedication in Latin[1], not Oscan.

Roman Names

*All male Roman citizens had three or four names. The first name or **praenomen** was the personal name used only by close friends and family. Common examples included Marcus, Gaius and Lucius.*

*The Middle name denoted the **gens** or clan to which the individual belonged.*

*Finally came the **cognomen** or the nickname. This was used to differentiate between different branches of each clan. Examples of nicknames included 'Caesar' (hairy) and 'Cicero' (chickpea).*

Women's names were more basic and usually a feminised version of their father's clan. However, if there were several daughters, this could become confusing. So it was common practice to add a further name to denote the order of birth, i.e, "first", "second", "third", or "big" and "little".

Figure 20: Statue of Apollo facing the cella of the temple

A final example of Roman dominance over Pompeii can be found in the Capitolium, whose ruins still dominate the northern edge of the forum.

∼

10
THE CAPITOLIUM

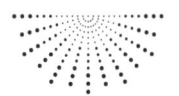

Figure 21: Capitoline Temple Today

THE ORIGINAL *CAPITOLIUM* WAS BUILT ON THE CAPITOLINE HILL IN Rome. It was dedicated to the principal Roman deities of Jupiter Best and Greatest, Juno and Minerva. From the first years of the republic, the *Capitolium* was where consuls sacrificed every New Year, state officials took their vows, and triumphal sacrifices were made. The *Capitolium* was the religious and civic heart of Rome.

Every city that became Roman received *a Capitolium* to mark their association with Rome. Pompeii was no exception. The site chosen for the *Capitolium* in the town was at the head of the forum, where a second-century temple dedicated to Jupiter was already situated. The Romans razed this temple to the ground, leaving nothing but the podium. This now became the basis of their new temple.

Figure 22: Layout of the Capitolium. A. Cella, B. Tripartite podium for statues, C. Pronaos or courtyard, D. Platform for altar.

The previous temple had consisted of a single-roomed *cella* that housed the statue of the god. The *cella* of the new Capitolium was subdivided into three to accommodate the trio of cult statues. The interior was decorated with second style wall paintings and mosaic floors. Meanwhile outside, the *cella* entrance was framed by an imposing, two-story-high row of columns. All of this ensured the new temple dominated the forum with its imposing style.

But not every new structure dating from the colonial period emphasised Pompeii's conquest by Rome. The forum baths at VII.5.24 were a sign of Roman beneficence. Leave the forum by the Via del Foro. The baths are on the left-hand side of the road.

11
NEW CIVIC AMENITIES

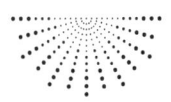

THE FORUM BATHS

Figure 23: Entrance to the Men's Section of the Forum Baths.

POMPEII ALREADY HAD A BATHHOUSE, THE STABIAN BATHS, SITUATED to the southeast of the forum. But the addition of 2000 plus citizens after the take over by Rome meant that the town's bathing facilities became overstretched. The need for new baths was so great that the Forum Baths were built at the expense of the city council, using the *"pequnia publica"*, the public purse, rather than the bank box of a wealthy donor.

Did You Know?.....

Contrary to popular opinion, Roman Baths were not the cleanest of places. When it came to draining used bathwater, it was not simply a matter of pulling out a plug. Consequently, baths were full of dirt and bacteria — especially as they had multiple users.

According to Marcus Aurelius, "oil, sweat, dirt, filthy water, all things disgusting"[1] were part and parcel of the Roman bathing experience.

Figure 24: Plan of the Forum Baths. A. Men's Entrance, B. Women's Entrance, C. Shops, D. Palaestra, E. Men's Apodyterium, F. Men's Frigidarium, G. Men's Tepidarium, H. Men's Caldarium, I. Women's Apodyterium with cold basin, J. Women's Caldarium, K. Women's Tepidarium, L. Furnace.

Rooms of the Bathhouse

Apodyterium — *the Changing Room*
Tepidarium — *the Warm Room*
Caldarium — *the Hot Room*
Frigidarium —*the Cold Room, which included a cold plunge bath.*

The new baths were state of the art. Fronted by shops and apartments, they split into male and female sections, each equipped with latrines and the usual bathing facilities. The baths also had a *palaestra* for exercising and an *apodyterium* or changing room, lit by a bronze framed window, complete with a half-inch thick pane of glass. The frame had two pivots, meaning it was possible to open the window and ventilate the baths.

Bathing usually occurred in the late afternoon and early evening, so the bathhouse needed lamps for extra illumination — especially in the winter months. Over 500 oil lamps were found in a corridor of the Forum Baths. Their light brightened the richly decorated rooms — but the smoke they created also blackened the walls and ceilings. Much of this decoration is hard to appreciate today, although the image below gives some idea of what it would have looked like.

DISCOVERING POMPEII

Figure 25: The Decor in the Tepidarium

∼

Roman Toilets

Roman toilets did not consist of separate cubicles but were vast open spaces where users could converse and read while relieving themselves in public. Wastewater from the baths constantly flowed under the rows of stone seats, flushing away patron's waste.

∼

Figure 26: A Roman Hypocaust

Heating the Bathhouse

The heating systems of bathhouses were constructed as follows. First, tiles were laid at ground level to form the base for two-foot pillars of eight-inch bricks set at regular intervals. Warm air created by the bathhouse furnace would circulate between these brick pillars, warming the bathhouse floor, which was created by laying two-foot tiles on top of this hypocaust system.[2]

Vitruvius and Bathhouses

According to Vitruvius, bathhouses were built in the warmest positions possible, ideally facing south to make the most of natural light and warmth.

Although men and women bathed separately, their hot rooms needed to be next to each other so they could share the same furnace for heating water. Bathhouse water was stored in three cylinders: one for the hot room, one for the warm room and one for the cold room. The cylinders were all interlinked so that once the water had flowed out of the hot room cylinder, it was replaced by water from the tepid room cylinder, which was restocked by the cold room supply.[3]

The new baths benefitted all Pompeians, old and new alike. The Temple of Augustan Fortune, just across the street at VII.4.1, shows how other Roman institutions could be equally socially inclusive.

12
SLAVES AND CIVIC RELIGION

THE TEMPLE OF AUGUSTAN FORTUNE.

Figure 27: The Remains of the Temple of Augustan Fortune

THE CULT OF AUGUSTAN FORTUNE WAS JUST ONE OF THE MANY dedicated to the emperor Augustus during the early imperial period. Although Augustus was not yet deified, the imperial cult allowed the people of the empire to show their loyalty to his *genius* or spirit.

Besides being dedicated to the spirit of a living man rather than a god, the cult was unique in one other way: slaves and freedmen ministered to it. Usually, priests were local dignitaries or politicians. Their religious appointment went hand in hand with their public role. Those of servile origin could not hold public office. Freedmen could not stand for election, only their sons. Slaves usually had no role in religion beyond acting as servants to priests.

～

Roman Slavery

Slaves were an essential part of Roman life. They worked on the land, home, industry, and trade. Approximately one in three of the Italian population during the imperial period were enslaved.

No one debated the rights and wrongs of owning another person as, to the Romans, slavery was an accepted part of the natural order. Most slaves were captives or the descendants of captives. As these people had been defeated and subjugated, it was natural that they would fall under the dominium or mastery of the Roman victors.

Varro described slaves as talking tools[1]. They had no rights in Roman society. They could not marry or have a legally recognised family. They could not own property and any money they held was at the discretion of their master. They could be restrained, beaten and even killed at their master's whim — although laws were eventually passed to prevent excessive and unjustified cruelty, such as Gaius, 53, which stated that:

" By a constitution of the Most Holy Emperor Antoninus, anyone who kills his slave, without good reason, is not less liable than one who kills the slave of another; and the excessive harshness of masters is restrained by another constitution of the same Emperor; ...... slaves who flee for refuge to the temples of the Gods or the statues of the Emperor, ordered that if the cruelty of masters appeared to be intolerable, they should be compelled to sell their slaves" [2]

～

Figure 28: Roman relief of a Priestess, accompanied by a slave, performing a sacrifice

The temple of Augustan Fortune in Pompeii was manned by freedmen *magistri*, assisted by slave *ministri*. This innovation allowed the servile classes a role in public life. However, it was costly for those involved. Each slave was required to contribute to an annual statue base to signify their dedication to the cult. But the bases recorded their names, allowing slaves a similar public immortality to that of local politicians.

Manumission

Slaves could achieve freedom. A master could allow them to save to buy their freedom (although technically, the slave could not own money). Alternatively, a master could free a slave — manumit them — either during his lifetime or under the terms of his will.

However, a manumitted slave, as a freedman, could never be a citizen. He could not hold political office and, despite his newfound freedom, remained bound to his former master, now as a client rather than a slave. As a client, the freedman remained obliged to his former master and could even be re-enslaved if he was deemed disrespectful.

However, despite these disadvantages, many former slaves prospered and even became wealthy and powerful.

∼

A Marcus Tullius built the temple of Augustan Fortune on his own land and at his own expense in the last years of the first century BC. Tullius had been a *duumvir* and an *augur* and was honoured by Augustus as a military tribune. But unlike civic donors from the early years of Pompeii's Roman period, Tullius was not a Roman incomer but a local Pompeian.

∼

The Roman Imperial period marked a general revival in the fortunes of Pompeii's old elite. This is demonstrated by the next stopping point, next to the shrine of the public Lares at VII.9.3

∼

13
POMPEII'S PARDON

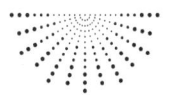

THE AUGUSTAN FORUM

Figure 29: Centre of the Augustan Forum with the Travertine marble slabs exposed

POLITICIANS IN POMPEII HAD ALWAYS NEEDED WEALTH TO COMPETE for public office. Money was needed to finance the entertainments, doles and public works that would win over the electorate. However, the fines imposed on the elite after the conquest of Pompeii meant that although they were not barred from office, they simply couldn't afford to take part in public life. However, Caesar's pardon of Pompeii released the old elite from the burden of financial penalties.

Pompeii's Pardon

On becoming dictator of the Roman State in 48BC, Julius Caesar pardoned all the combatants of the Social War. All suppression of and restraints on the old Italic elites were removed. Pompeii's aristocracy was free to govern once more.

~

By the early imperial period, elite Pompeians were back in business and busy making their mark on the forum once again. The Rufii, an important old Pompeian family who had made their money in wine, extensively renovated the Sanctuary of Apollo. An altar was set up in the centre of the forum and statues were added to its southern end. Even the old tufa paving stones were replaced with travertine marble. The donor made sure no one forgot who had paid for this; the commemorative inscription stretched the whole width of the forum.

Even shopping became monumental. The second century BC **macellum** or market was given a face-lift and adorned with grand collonaded porticos and statues.

Figure 30: Layout of the macellum. A. Entrances, B. Colonnaded Portico, C. Fish Market, D. Large Market, E. Shops/money lending booths, F. Sheep pens, G. Shrine to the Imperial Family, H. Rows of shops.

Five shops have been identified in the façade of the *macellum*, which were possibly moneychanger's booths (E). Inside was an open courtyard, edged with a roofed collonaded portico, painted with images of food, wine and the Goddess Vesta as the patron of millers and bakers (B).

In the centre was a covered circular pavilion (C). The pavilion was part of the fish market, as evidenced by fish scales and bones in the drain surrounding the structure[1]. The fish were cleaned on a nearby marble slab while water from a central fountain washed them and kept them fresh. They were then sold from one of 11 shops to the southwest of the *macellum* in an area shaded from the sun (H).

On the north side were twelve more stalls. Based on archaeological remains, they were selling a variety of grocery items: grapes, plums, lentils, chestnuts, figs, wheat, bread, mutton and goat.

Figure 31: Reconstruction of the macellum

∾

But the ambitions of the elite now went beyond Pompeii. They were looking to impress Rome, as was demonstrated by the building next door to the macellum, The Temple of the Public Lares.

∾

14
THE IMPERIAL CULT

THE TEMPLES OF THE PUBLIC LARES AND VESPASIAN

Figure 32: Layout of the Temple of the Public Lares. A. Apse, B. Courtyard, C. Ala, D. Altar.

IN THE EARLY IMPERIAL PERIOD, THE SHOPS AND HOUSES ALONG THIS eastern edge of the forum were demolished and the final phase of civic building began. Two of these new buildings were temples: The Temple of the Public Lares and the temple of Vespasian. Like the temple of Augustan Fortune, these new temples celebrated the cult of Rome's emperor and were erected by elite Pompeians, eager to show their loyalty to the Imperial regime. Both temples were based on Roman religious ideals and used decorative language designed to aggrandise the imperial family.

To the left is the Temple of the Public Lares. Unlike the neighbouring temple of Vespasian and the Eumachia building, it lacks repairs to its fabric. This suggests it was built after the earthquake of 62AD[1].

~

The Lares

The exact nature of the Lares is debatable. Ovid believed they were descended from a nymph, while other Romans maintained the Lares were actually the ancestral dead, guarding their descendants.

It is probably best to see Lares as urbanised nature spirits for they were essentially spirits of the land. They remained on their plots even after vegetation was cleared and buildings were erected, simply absorbing new constructs and occupants under their guardianship.

In a town such as Pompeii, a particular Lares' territory could encapsulate a particular district, or-as in the case of the public Lares, the town as a whole.

~

In the centre of the Temple of the Public Lares was an altar dedicated to the guardian spirits of Pompeii. But the walls of the temple were lined with *Alae* that contained statues of the imperial family.

Figure 33: Layout of the Temple of Vespasian. A. Entrance, B. Courtyard, C. Vestibule, D. Altar, E. Cella, F. Tetrastyle Porch, G. Storerooms and priest rooms.

To the right is the Temple of Vespasian. This is more properly the Temple of Augustus, as this was who it was originally dedicated to. The temple bears the emblems of Augustus, voted to him by the Senate in 27BC: the shield, the oak wreath, laurel garlands and a sacrificed bull.

This display to honour the emperor was not without ulterior motive. The donors, no doubt, hoped that they would attract imperial recognition and favour. For politically ambitious individuals with the right friends, there was a world open to them beyond Pompeii's City government: Rome itself.

∽

Roman architecture in general was very much the model for this later phase of building as the Eumachia Building next door at VII.9.1 demonstrates.

∽

15
WOMEN IN POMPEII

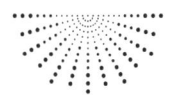

THE EUMACHIA BUILDING

Figure 34: Entrance to the Eumachia Building

THE EUMACHIA BUILDING WAS NAMED AFTER A PUBLIC PRIESTESS and local business woman who dedicated the building on behalf of herself and her son Marcus Numistrius Fronto-probably as a gift to the city to further Fronto's election prospects.

Who Was Eumachia?

A highly successful and wealthy woman, Eumachia held land and property in her own right. Eumachia's family, however, were not part of the old, established Pompeian elite. Her father, Lucius Eumachius made a fortune from his brick manufacturer business which allowed his daughter to marry into one of the old elite families, the Numistrii Frontones. No doubt Eumachia's new husband's family welcomed the fresh injection of cash into their coffers after the early punitive years under Rome.

Figure 35: Statue of Eumachia.

Eumachius seems to have been well respected, as most inscriptions Eumachia set up identified her as his daughter, rather than naming her husband. Marcus Numistrius Fronto had been a duumvir of Pompeii in 3AD and was so a prominent man. However, by the time Eumachia began to make her civic dedications, his name was nowhere to be seen. This was probably because Eumachia was now a widow. However, it also suggests she was looking for her own public role.

By now, Eumachia had become a public priestess, the only civic role open to a woman. She had also started financing her own civic monuments, including the famous Eumachia Building. This building was constructed to enhance the political prospects of Eumachia's son, Marcus Numistrius Fronto the younger.

*"**Eumachia, daughter of Lucius, public priestess, in her own name and that of her son, Marcus Numistrius Fronto, built at her own expense, the chalcidicum, crypt and portico in honour of Augustan concord and piety and also dedicated them**," declared the inscription over the building's portico. Fronto Junior's name was prominent. However, there was no doubt who the people of Pompeii had to thank for the building.*

Eumachia was now a patron in her own right- and she was earning gratitude for it. At the back of the Eumachia building, in a central niche, a statue to the building's benefactress was set up by the fuller's guild. Whether this indicates Eumachia was involved in the cloth industry or had simply performed some service for the fuller's guild we will never know. However, she was significant enough to them to deserve a very public gesture of thanks.

Eumachia's tomb is the largest found in Pompeii so far. Situated outside the Nucerian gate, it was raised above the street and set back from a terraced area which includes seats for visiting mourners. It was a tomb designed to hold not only Eumachia but also her future descendants. Its size and construction indicate that Eumachia was a roman matron who believed she and she alone had established a legacy for her family that would last for generations to come.

∽

Some have speculated that the Eumachia building was a meeting hall for the fuller's guild. This is based on the plaque inside the building, dedicated to Eumachia by the fuller's guild in gratitude for her patronage. However, the Eumachia building bears an uncanny resemblance to the *Porticus Livae*, built in the Subura district of Rome in 7BC[1]. The *Porticus* was built by another influential mother with an up and coming son: the Empress Livia, wife of Augustus and mother of the future Emperor Tiberius.

Women in Roman Life

Roman women were not allowed to vote or act without the authority of a male guardian: their father, husband or any other male appointed to the role. In theory, this meant that a woman could only contract business with her guardian's consent.

Roman women were traditionally confined to the house. Here, the ideal Roman matron would care for and educate her children, manage her household and industriously occupy any spare moments with spinning and weaving.
However, during the Imperial Period, legal restraints were relaxed. The Emperor Claudius freed mothers of four children from the requirement of a male guardian, effectively giving them their independence.

However, even before this concession was made, there were plenty of women in Pompeii involved in business. One of fish sauce magnet Umbricius Scarus's workshops was managed by his freedwoman Umbricia Fortunata. Other notable Pompeii businesswomen included Julia Felix and Naevoleia Tyche who made a fortune from shipping.

Figure 36: Layout of the Eumachia Building. A. Entrance, B. Porch, C. Auction Niche, D. Niche for Statue, E. Cryptoporticus, F. Central Apse, G. Exedra containing Eumachia's statue.

Both the Eumachia building and the *Porticus Livae* were dedicated to Concordia Augusta. This shared goddess was not the only similarity the *Porticus* and Eumachia's building shared. Both had large colonnaded courtyards, two small side gardens and podiums for speakers flanking the main apse. These similarities suggest Eumachia was directly copying the *Porticus Livae*. The similarities in form suggest both would have had a similar function and so it is possible that the Eumachia Building was not simply a guild house but, like the *Porticus Livae*, it was a purpose built community/leisure centre.

The Eumachia Building also contains other architectural features directly copied from architecture in Rome. Within the *chalcidicum* or exterior porch was a copy of a statue of Romulus. The doorframe to the building was also edged with carvings of acanthus leaves identical to those found on the *Ara Pacis* or Altar of Peace set up by Augustus in the Roman forum.

The Eumachia Building, like most others in the forum was left in damage and disarray by the earthquake of 62AD. Most of these civic buildings were not fully repaired by the time of the eruption that destroyed the town. Those that were show that Pompeii's priorities had shifted. Town morale and hygiene now ranked above civic splendour, as the fully restored Amphitheatre and forum baths prove.

∼

Religion also remained important in Pompeii-but not the traditional, classical type. Return now to the Via del Tempio d'Iside for our next stopping point at VIII.7.28; The Temple of Isis.

∼

16
THE RISE OF THE MYSTERY CULT

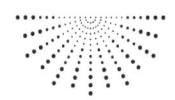

THE TEMPLE OF ISIS

Figure 37: Reconstruction of the Temple of Isis

THE TEMPLE OF ISIS WAS THE ONLY TEMPLE IN POMPEII TO BE FULLY restored after the earthquake. This is a testament to the importance of the cult to the town's life.

Isis had been a part of Pompeii's religious life for some time. The cult was probably introduced via trade links with Alexandria in the third or second century BC. It was around this period that the first temple was built. The temple's precinct impinged upon the large theatre, something that could only have occurred with the consent of the city council. Yet Isis was not a public cult or central to large civic festivals and sacrifices. Her temple had a small, enclosed precinct for private ceremonies. For Isis's cult was a mystery religion open only to devotees and initiates.

~

Mystery Cults of the Roman Empire.

Traditional Roman religion concentrated very much on the here and now rather than the afterlife. Health, wealth and good fortune were its primary concerns; whether of an individual, family or the state as a whole.

Unlike Roman religion, Mystery Cults combined worldly concerns along with hopes for the afterlife. Generally of eastern origin, these cults involved secret knowledge only revealed to initiates. The Cult of Isis was not the only popular mystery cult in the Roman empire. The cults of Mithras and Cybele are just two other examples.

~

Unlike regular Roman State religions, mystery cults concerned themselves with the afterlife. According to mythology, the goddess Isis had resurrected her husband Osiris from the dead. Isis's followers believed she could do the same for them. But the goddess also offered worldly benefits to her followers. She was a patron of sailors and a mother goddess figure. As a result, her cult was attractive to a wide social spectrum, including the wealthy, women and slaves.

Figure 38: Reconstruction of the Purgatorium

A prominent local freedman, Numerius Popidius Ampliatus, constructed the new temple to ensure the advancement of his young son. Isis's cult must have had a significant standing in Pompeii for him to choose the cult for such a gesture. Ampliatus's ploy worked. His son was elected a councillor at the age of six as a sign of the council's gratitude.

The new temple was beautifully reconstructed and decorated. Set on a high podium, it overlooked a courtyard with two altars and a shrine called a *Purgatorium* where worshippers could purify themselves with water from the River Nile. Inside, it was decorated with murals depicting idealised scenes of ancient Egypt. At the back was a special room for the performance of sacred plays.

~

Other Religions in Pompeii

Archaeology has also revealed evidence of other, less mainstream religions in Pompeii. They included:

Christianity: *An inscription including the word "Christianos" was discovered on the wall of an inn in Region VII*[1]

Judaism: *Aside from Jewish names in graffiti, there are various biblical references on the walls of Pompeii. One wall along the Via del Abbondanza includes the words "Sodoma Gomora," referring to the doomed- and licentious-biblical cities of Sodom and Gomorra. Pompeii's Jewish community must have been substantial as the garum industry was also producing kosher garum, if inscriptions found on two amphora are to be believed.*[2]

∾

However, despite being the location of the Cult of Isis, the Triangular Forum itself was, by the Roman period, no longer the heart of Pompeii. The Doric Temple was long disused and in ruins. However, the area was not wholly abandoned. It has been speculated that the area had become a parkland, a place where Pompeians and visitors alike could come to relax and gaze upon the picturesque ruins of Pompeii's past.

Rather as we do today.

∾

PART II
DAILY LIFE IN POMPEII

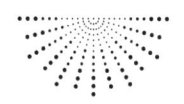

A WALK DOWN THE VIA DELL'ABBONDANZA

17
THE VIA DELL'ABBONDANZA

INTRODUCTION

Figure 39: Tour of Daily Life in Pompeii

The Tour

A. The Via dell'Abbondanza
   B. The Stabian Baths
   C. The Water Tower
   D. The House of Epodes Rufus

E. Stephanus's Fuller
F. The Cloth Merchant's Shop
G. The House of the Cryptoporticus
H. The House of Paquius Proculus
I. Asellina's Tavern
J. Ordinary Apartments
K. The Bakery of the Chaste Lovers
L. The House of Julius Polybius
M. The House of the Orchard
N. The House of Trebius Valens
O. The Site of the Armaturarum
P. The House of Octavius Quartius
Q. The House of the Marine Venus
R. The Properties of Julia Felix
S. A Pompeian Winery and Vineyards
T. The Amphitheatre.

~

The Roman name of the Via dell'Abbondanza is unknown. Its modern name is taken from the relief of an overflowing cornucopia carved on one of its street fountains. But the *'Street of Abundance'* is certainly an appropriate title for the road. For, from businesses to bread, houses and hygiene, gladiators, politics and wine, the Via dell'Abbondanza is packed with features that tell the story of the daily life and character of everyday Pompeii.

Figure 40: The Fountain of Abundance

∽

The western point of the Via dell' Abbondanza marks the end of the main forum, the public heart of Pompeii. It also marks the beginnings of the 'behind the scenes' life of the town.

The first roads in Pompeii were of simple beaten earth. But by the time the town became a roman colony, they were fully formed and the Via dell' Abbondanza had grown into the *Decumanus Maximus* or main road of the Roman town.

∽

Road Names in Pompeii

The names by which we know the roads of Pompeii are not the ones that its citizens would have used. An inscription near the **Stabian Gate** *does provide us with the Roman name of three Pompeian roads: The Jovia, Decuria and Pompeiana. We do not, however, know exactly which of the town's byways these names refer to.*

One road in Pompeii, however can be identified by its original name. That road is known today as the **Porto Ercolano** *however, its actual name was the* **Vera Safina**-*The Salt Gate, according to an Oscan inscription. The road took its name from its route out of the town and past the coastal salt-pans.*

∾

This starting point of the Via dell' Abbondanza was deceptively sedate. Traffic would have been sparse, possibly because this end of the road acted as a ceremonial way between the town's main and triangular *fora*. However, as it ran eastwards through Pompeii, past the junction with the Via Stabiana and into the town centre, before terminating at the Sarno Gate, the Via dell'Abbondanza became much more lively.

∾

Main Roman Roads

Decumanus(i). Refers to main roads orientated from east to west. The main decumanus in a Roman town was known as the Decumanus Maximus.

Decumani ran perpendicular to **Cardines**, with each Cardo running from north to south. The main cardo was known as the **Cardo Maximus**.

Decumani in Pompeii:
   Via di Nola
   Via delle Fortuna
   Via del Abbondanza (The Decumanus Maximus)

Cardines in Pompeii:
  Via Stabiana *(The Cardo Maximus)*
  Via di Mercurio
  Via del Foro
  Via delle Scule
  Via di Nocera

Figure 41: Pompeii's Main Roads

∼

Along this stretch of the Via dell Abbondanza, two storey buildings, plastered and painted red and white and daubed with graffiti flanked a road which was now jammed with carts and pack animals competing for right of way. On the pavements, people jostled for space, dodging children, beggars and other passers-by. They may have stopped to browse the wares of the small *tabernae* or shops, sandwiched between homes and businesses-or to buy a much needed cup of wine.

Street life on the Via dell' Abbondanza was hot, noisy and smelly. But at least the densely packed buildings, along with the shop awnings and balconies of apartments above would have offered some shade to the busy street.

But people could escape the streets to refresh themselves with a bath. Perhaps they visited the Stabian Baths found at the junction with the Via Stabiana in Region VII.1.8.

18
PUBLIC BATHING

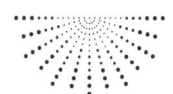

THE STABIAN BATHS

Figure 42: Plan of the Stabian Baths. THE WOMEN'S BATHS: A. Apodyterium, B. Tepidarium, C. Caldarium. THE MEN'S BATHS: D. Caldarium, E. tepidarium, F. Apodyterium, G. Laconium. GENERAL ROOMS: H. Private Rooms, I. Latrines, J. shops, K. Palestra, L. Main Entrance, M. Swimming Pool, N. Side Entrance.

Public baths in Pompeii were free. Essentially, they were large leisure complexes where rich and poor could escape city life, exercise, and enjoy a long soak.

∽

Seneca and Public Bath Houses:

'The hubbub makes you sorry that you are not deaf. I hear the beefcake boys wheezing and grunting as they lift their lead weights and the masseur's hand's slapping their shoulders.

Then the ball players arrive and start yelling out the score-that's usually all I can take.

But there's also those people who plunge themselves into the water with an almighty splash and that only gives a mild idea of what goes on.

At least these people have normal voices. Apart from them there is the depilator who screeches for customers and never shuts up until he's stripping the hair from someone's armpits and making them yell even louder than he does.

Then there is the drinks peddler and the sausage salesman and all the other hucksters, each bawling in his own special way[1].

∽

As can be seen from Seneca's description, bathhouses were busy- and noisy-places! People not only went to wash but to exercise, enjoy a massage and beauty treatments as well as relax, read and talk with friends.

∽

Did You Know?...

Men and women bathed at different times. Women went to the baths early in the day while men went in the afternoon when they had concluded their day's work.

～

There were three main bathhouses in Pompeii. The oldest, built in the second century BC were the Stabian Baths, found on the left of the Via dell' Abbondanza. Through the entrance was a large colonnaded exercise yard, complete with a swimming pool, where patrons could enjoy a workout before bathing.

The baths themselves were split into male and female zones. Each had the same facilities: changing rooms and a series of cold, warm and hot rooms. The women's baths were smaller and entered from a back street. The larger men's baths were accessed from this road.

～

Did You Know?....

In 79AD, only the women's section of the Stabian Baths was in use. The rest of the baths were under repair.

～

The Stabian Baths preserve many features lost from later Roman bathhouses. In particular, they have private bathing rooms, (marked 'H' on the plan). These may have been used by couples who wanted to use them for more than a secluded wash!

∼

Did You Know?...

According to Seneca, people didn't visit the bathhouse everyday. Most visited once or twice a week. It was usual to have a quick wash down at home especially first thing in the morning.

∼

The Romans updated the Stabian Baths once Pompeii became a colony. Perhaps the most significant of their improvements was to switch the water supply from the uncertain local wells to the Naples aqueduct.

∼

Part of that new water distribution system is just in front of you, at the crossroads between the Via dell Abbondanza and the Via Stabiana.

∼

19
POMPEII'S WATER SUPPLY

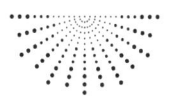

THE WATER TOWER

Figure 43: Water Tower on the Via dell'Abbondanza

THE NEW CITY WATER SUPPLY WAS BUILT AT THE END OF THE FIRST century BC. It was ingenious. It was fed with water from the Augustan aqueduct which was collected in a central reservoir, the *castellum aqua* at the highest point of the city, near to the Vesuvian Gate. From here, the water was divided into three large lead pipes and distributed around Pompeii.

Did You Know?..

Recent analysis of the teeth of people from ancient Pompeii shows they were healthy and strong. This is probably due to the local water supply, which is naturally rich in fluoride.

∽

Although the water was moving downhill from the *castellum aqua*, some areas of Pompeii were at different elevations to others. This meant the water pressure also varied across the city-and in some areas it was too high. So to resolve this, fourteen six-metre high *castella secundaria* or secondary water towers were built, such as the one shown in the photograph.

Piping water up the tower into a tank de-pressurised it. The water was then piped down the tower, under the pavements and into pipes which supplied private houses, baths and water fountains with fresh water[1].

Figure 44: Ornamental Fountain from the House of the Small Fountain, Pompeii.

∽

But a free flowing water supply caused other problems. At IX.1.20 is the House of Epidius Rufus, which is on the left side of the road just past the water tower. Here you'll discover why.

~

20

THE STATE OF THE STREETS

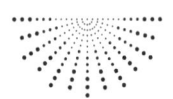

THE HOUSE OF EPIDIUS RUFUS.

Figure 45: Street View of the House of Epidius Rufus. Note the extra elevation above the public pavement

POMPEII'S STREETS WOULD NOT HAVE BEEN AS CLEAN AS THEY appear today. Unfortunately, the one thing the Romans didn't equip their new colony with was an efficient sewage system.

Although the main forum, the bathhouses and the palestra were all served by a drainage system, this did not extend to the rest of the town. Instead, rainfall and the downward slope of the streets was relied upon to flush out waste through the town gates.

But despite Pompeii's natural downward slope, its streets often flooded with the overspill from water towers and fountains. So various measures were employed to try and mitigate this flooding. The entrances of some side streets were raised above that of the main road, to prevent rainwater from flowing into them, while at the city gates, drains were dug to prevent water accumulating[1].

But rainfall and overspills could not be relied upon to keep the streets clean-and the streets of Pompeii were filthy! Household waste, manure from draft animals and the usual litter of any town meant the roads were a mire. This, plus the waste from butchers, tanners and even people's chamber pots meant that the road could be a smelly and unpleasant place.

So it's no wonder pavements could be up to a metre high in places[2]. Nor is it difficult to understand why pedestrians needed stepping stones to cross the road.

Some owners of the larger houses clearly felt the pavements were not high enough. The house of Epidius Rufus, built in the late second century BC, belonged to an old Pompeian family. The Rufii elevated the entrance of their house a further metre above the street. The result was their own private pavement, making the Rufii, literally, as well as metaphorically 'above' everyone who passed their home.

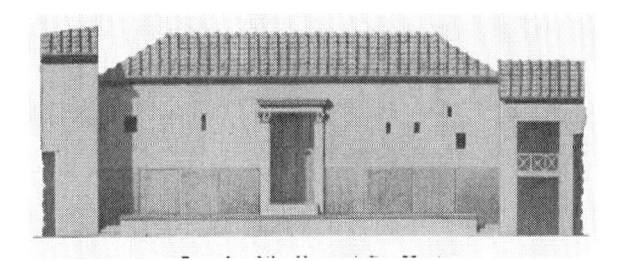

Figure 46: Reconstruction of the exterior of the House of Epidius Rufus

The House of Epidius Rufus

Also known as the House of the Diadumeni, the House of Epidius Rufus was an old style Pompeian house built in the late second century BC.

Besides being built on a raised terrace above the pavement, the house had several other unusual features. Firstly, it had a triple entrance facing the street. Visitors would have entered through the front doors, but then instead of entering the atrium directly, they were filtered down a corridor to the right. It seems that the atrium's double doors would only have been opened to receive large groups of visitors.

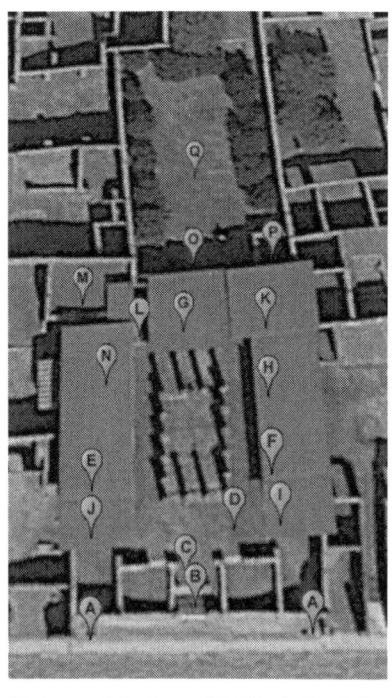

Figure 47: Layout of the House of Epidius Rufus. A. Steps to the raised pavement, B. Vestibule, C. Fauces, D. Atrium, E. Ala, F. Ala, G. Tablinium, H. Cubicula, I. Cubicula, J. Cubicula, K. Triclinium, L. Andron, M. Service Area, N. Stairs, O. Colonnade, P. Garden Room, Q. Garden.

The atrium (D) was the centre of the house, an elaborate court like room edged by a Corinthian colonnade of doric columns-one of only four examples of such colonnades found in Pompeii. The central impluvium was equally dramatic and was equipped with an ornamental fountain which threw a jet of water into the central pool.

Surrounding the atrium were small cubicula (H, I, J). These were possibly used as bedrooms for family members despite the fact that the atrium was a very public place. Behind the atrium was the main triclinium or dining room (K) and the master's tablinium or study (G). Both of these rooms overlooked a colonnaded walkway (O) which in its turn edged the old fashioned hortus (Q) which occupied the rest of the property, instead of a peristyle garden.

Maybe the Rufii were trying to distance themselves from the neighbours as well as the street. That's understandable when you consider townhouses could be next door to a small trade or industry. One can be found nearby, at I. 6.7 - the Fullery of Stephanus.

21
TRADE AND INDUSTRY

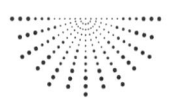

STEPHANUS'S FULLERY

Figure 48: Exterior of Stephanus's Fullery

THE CLOTH INDUSTRY WAS A VITAL PART OF THE POMPEIAN economy and fulleries marked the final stage in the cloth making processes. They also doubled as local launderettes. The building on the right is Stephanus's Fullery, the best preserved of the seventeen fullers uncovered so far in Pompeii and one of the largest. We know the owners name from the electoral notice: '*Stephanus rogat...*' 'Stephanus recommends...' painted on its façade.

The Fullery Trade

The processing and finishing of cloth was a profitable trade in Pompeii. When Stephanus's fullery was excavated, a number of bodies were found behind its locked entrance. One was clutching a bag of gold and silver coins worth around 1090 sesterces-roughly $1090 or £780.

Stephanus's fullery began its life as a house. However, after the earthquake of 62AD it was converted into a fuller. While living quarters were maintained upstairs, on the ground floor, the entrance was widened to allow carts to access the former atrium of the house. The atrium's *impluvium,* was also converted into a giant washing basin.

Figure 49: The Converted Impluvium

The smelly business of treating and finishing cloth was carried out in the former peristyle at the back of the building. Here, cloth was processed by treating it with carbonate of soda, potash, fuller's earth and urine. The latter was collected from passers-by who 'made a donation' in a pottery vessel placed in the street.

Figure 50: Fresco of Workers hanging clothes to dry

The pictures show some of the fulling processes. After being treated and washed, cloth would be hung to dry from beams in the peristyle. Then it was 'ironed' in a wooden, screw operated clothes press. A final finishing treatment was then applied which consisted of an application of sulphur to whiten the cloth. This final touch was added after the cloth was wrapped around a cylindrical frame-as the final picture shows. This picture also shows how cloth was carded to give it a neat finish.

Figure 51: Fresco showing the Whitening Process

∼

Pompeii's Textile Industry

The evidence preserved by the eruption of 79AD shows that Pompeii had a thriving textile industry. Electoral graffiti shows the strength of influence wielded by the textile workers of the town. The walls of Pompeii are full of recommendations from fullers and dyers, as well as felt and wool makers-suggesting that they had an economic strength that made them a force to be reckoned with.

*Fulleries aside, commercial textile workshops have been found spread across various districts of Pompeii. Some were **Officinae Lanifricariae**- wool processing workshops, which were concentrated in the area east of the forum in what was the ancient version of an industrial park. Elsewhere across the town were commercial **Textinae**-places for spinning and weaving as well as **Officinae Tinctoria**- dye workshops.*

∼

Stephanus's Fullery was clearly profitable. But to the people of Pompeii, a successful business depended as much on the will of the gods as hard work. A couple of buildings along, on the other side of the road at IX.7.5-6, is a shop that demonstrates the importance of religion in daily life.

∽

22
POPULAR RELIGION

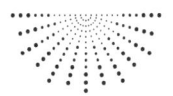

THE CLOTH MERCHANT'S SHOP

Figure 52: Shrine to the Lares in Pompeii

RELIGION WAS AN INTEGRAL PART OF EVERYDAY LIFE IN POMPEII. Good luck phallic symbols were carved on the tufa blocks paving the road. A shrine marked each crossroads, similar to those of saints in catholic countries. In Pompeii, they were dedicated to the guardian spirits of each district, the Lares. Thirty such shrines have been identified in Pompeii-some complete with ash, burnt wood and the remains of sacrifices made at the time of the eruption.

~

The Pax Deorum

*Roman religion was based on the Pax Deorum or **"the peace of the gods".** This meant that, so long as the gods received their dues in the form of correctly performed rituals and sacrifices, they would be content and continue to protect the Roman community they represented; be that an individual home, town or the whole of the Empire.*

However, if the gods were unhappy, they would show their anger through nature. Signs of divine displeasure could include lightening strikes, natural disasters or just plain bad luck.

~

These local shrines consisted of an altar, which was often decorated and inscribed. Common motifs included pictures of the Lares, a snake representing the district's *genius loci*, and pictures of the shrine's attendants. These attendants were generally low status individuals. Freedmen acted as *magistri* at shrines while slaves were assisting *ministri*.

These symbols and roadside altars were not signs of faith and devotion, as we understand them. Roman religion was more pragmatic; a god's favour had to be earned and duly recognised if it was received. It was a belief system based on duty and mutual respect-not abasement and love.

∼

Examples of Religious Graffiti:

"By the Sacred Lares, I ask you....." (request daubed next to a shrine.)

"Be on your guard against evil or else if you disregard this, you may incur the wrath of Jupiter[1]."

This highly pragmatic attitude to religion may well explain the murals on the outside of this shop. A woman is selling cloth on the lower panel of the first image, suggesting the shop was a cloth merchants. Above her is Mercury in his capacity as the god of trade, leaving a temple with a loaded purse. Was this the shop owner's way of attracting custom? The murals suggest he was a business worth patronising because he had the favour of the gods.

Figure 53: Mercury Leaving a Temple (Mural on the Clothworker's shop)

The second picture depicts Venus Pompeiana, the patron goddess of the town. To the Pompeians, she was not the Roman goddess of love but a much older deity associated with luck and prosperity. A fitting patron for a successful Pompeian merchant.

Figure 54: Venus Pompeiana

∾

Prosperous businesses must have financed many of the fine houses along the Via dell' Abbondanza. The house at the next stopping point, across the road at I.6.2, may have been one.

∾

23
INNOVATIVE HOUSING

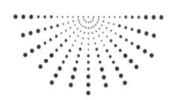

THE HOUSE OF THE CRYPTOPORTICUS.

Figure 55: Old Photograph of the Cryptoporticus c. 1914.

MOST ROMAN TOWN HOUSES CONFORMED TO THE STANDARD Vitruvian house plan. Entering from the street, a visitor would be led via a narrow passage to the atrium. The first room visible from the atrium was the *tablinium* or study, through which the client or casual visitor to the house might just catch a glimpse of the central *peristyle* garden. It was around this area that the private rooms of the house; the family rooms and dining and entertaining areas, were arranged.

∼

The Impluvium and Compluvium

*Two of the key features of the atrium or entrance hall of the Roman house was the **impluvium** and **compluvium**. These features originate from the time when the atrium was the main room of the home, where meals were eaten and work was done.*

Rainwater was an important resource and the impluvium and compluvium played a key role in its collection. The compluvium-the rectangular opening in the atrium roof allowed water in. The rain was then collected in the impluvium-the pool just below the compluvium. This was then stored in a water cistern underneath the atrium floor

---

∼

However, Vitruvius was also very clear that it was essential for an architect to modify house plans to suit the site[1]. This is exactly what happened at the House of the Cryptoporticus.

The House of the Cryptoporticus is an unusual and innovative house, which shows how money and imagination could overcome the lie of the land. One of the largest and finest house of late republican Pompeii, it is built on a slope, making it difficult for the plot to accommodate the full range of rooms required by a wealthy household. To overcome this, a terrace was added behind the atrium, increasing the ground floor. But instead of supporting this terrace with infill, the owner built a set of rooms into the space below it.

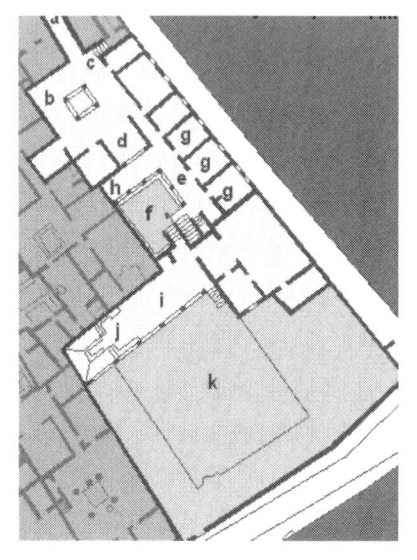

Figure 56: Plan of the first floor of the House of the Cryptoporticus

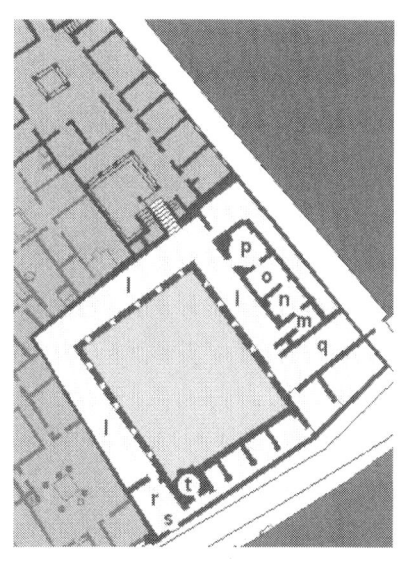

Figure 57: Plan of the 'underground suite' including the cryptoporticus (marked l on the plan)

The decorative scheme of this underground extension dates it to around 40BC. The area seems to have been designed as a novel dining and entertaining area. Guests descended into the underground suite of rooms by a set of steps near the small peristyle garden. This led onto the vaulted corridor or **cryptoporticus**, which gives the house its name. By day, the cryptoporticus was illuminated by skylights set high in its walls that were level with the garden. At night, it was lit with lamps. The corridor led onto to a magnificently decorated dining room and bath suite. In its heyday, the cryptoporticus would certainly have made an impression on anyone invited to dinner.

Late in the house's life, its status diminished. The House of the Cryptoporticus was divided into two properties and the cryptoporticus and its luxury baths were now reduced to storage areas.

But Pompeian householders wanted to impress clients and casual callers as well as their friends as demonstrated by the property next door at I.7.1. It belonged to Paquius Proculus, a man of means who needed a house to match.

∼

24
INTERIOR DESIGN

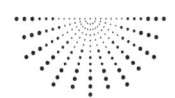

THE HOUSE OF PAQUIUS PROCULUS.

Figure 58: The atrium of the House of Paquius Proculus. Note the false doors in the walls, used to create the illusion of a larger house.

PAQUIUS PROCULUS WAS A MAN OF MEANS-SO MUCH SO THAT HE could afford to go into politics. Election notices on the façade of his house show that he stood for the office of *duumvir*, one of the two chief magistrates of Pompeii. More graffiti daubed on the exterior of the arena tells us that he won. Proculus was now an influential man.

The Election Graffiti of Paquius Proculus

"Thalamus, his client elects Publius Paquius Proculus duumvir with judicial power."

"All Pompeian's have elected Publius P Proculus duumvir with judicial power, worthy of public office." (wall of the amphitheatre.)[1]

Who was Paquius Proculus?

The case of Paquius Proculus illustrates the care needed when trying to recreate the lives of people who lived in Pompeii. Election notices mentioning his name were found on another house in Pompeii, besides this one on the Via dell Abbondanza. This second residence lies to the west, in Region VII of the city, an area between the Via Stabiana and the forum. It was this building that archaeologists initially believed to be Proculus's house.

The house contained plenty of information about the life and livelihood of its owner, which was used to create a lively narrative for the life of Proculus. A bakery was directly connected to the main residence and was presumed to be the owner's business. So, Paquius Proculus became a wealthy baker who used the money he had earned from his trade to finance his political career. Archaeologists could even say what he looked like, because of a portrait of the baker and his wife found on the premises. This was naturally assumed to be that of Proculus.

However, neither the house nor the portrait belonged to Paquius Proculus. For more graffiti found inside the house, conclusively identified the residence, the bakery and the portrait as belonging to a man, called Terentius Neo. As for The House of Paquius Proculus, there is no evidence to suggest that it belongs to anyone other than the person whose electoral notices adorn its façade. However, it also gives no clues as to how Proculus accumulated the wealth to finance his political career.

～

However Paquius Proculus made his money, his house let him down. The roman house was not just a home; it was also an office. The atrium was the main reception room of the house and needed to reinforce its owner's social status. Although Proculus's home had an expansive peristyle garden and a range of private rooms at the back (F-J on the plan), its frontage was small and narrow. The atrium took up all the available space. This meant clients and colleagues were received in an unimpressive reception area, which diminished the standing of the owner.

～

Roman Decorative Schemes.

The decorative styles used in Pompeii's houses and public buildings were grouped into four main types by Augusto Mau:

First Style:
(Masonry/Incrustation)
200-80BC. Created the illusion of marble slabs.

Second Style:
(Architectural Style)
80-30BC. Used emblems from public architecture in a domestic setting.

Third Style:
(Ornamental Style)
30BC-45AD. Panels of colour bordered with delicate motifs and pictures of gardens and landscapes.

Fourth Style:
(Fantastic/Illusory Style)
45AD onwards. Mythical and theatrical imagery.

Proculus overcame the problem of his atrium with decor. Firstly, he had his atrium painted with fashionable third style frescos. The walls were painted with panels of colour, each with a small picture or motif at their centre. Then, like so many politicians, he created a fake impression. On either side of the room, door shaped niches were added to suggest that more rooms and corridors ran off from the atrium. This made his house look more substantial than it actually was, supporting its owner's standing as one of Pompeii's leading citizens.

Figure 59: Layout of the House of Paquius Proculus. A. Fauces, B. Atrium, C. Cubicula, D. Tablinium, E. Walkway, F. Peristyle. G. Garden, H. Summer Triclinium, I. Oecus. J. Triclinium

∽

It is unlikely that the upwardly mobile Proculus or any of his friends would have frequented the next stopping point, just across the road at IX.2.2, a red and white painted building known as Asellina's tavern.

∽

25
EAT, DRINK AND BE MERRY

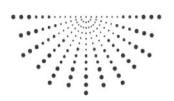

ASELLINA'S TAVERN.

Figure 60: The frontage of Asellina's tavern

POMPEII'S TAVERNS WERE A VITAL PART OF LIFE FOR ORDINARY citizens. Here, they could eat out or buy a hot takeaway meal. Taverns were also where they went for a good night out. A lamp lit caupona was the place to go for a drink and a game of dice, for gambling was a popular Roman pastime. Losers could always drown their sorrows in a beaker or two of the rough but cheap house wine. And if they were lucky, they could celebrate with

Falernian wine for around 4 as (just under half a denarius or two sestertii).

~

Types of Bars and Eateries:

Caupona/Taberna-*a food bar, often with lodgings for guests.*

Hospitium/Stabulum-*a guesthouse*

Copo-*A bar with seating*

Popina-*A type of low class 'pub' offering food and drink.*

~

Asellina's tavern is just one of the bars along the Via dell' Abbondanza. It was a *caupona*, which offered food, drink and possibly lodging to its patrons. The upper storey has not survived but the layout of the lower floor was clear to see before bombing during World War II damaged the *caupona*.

The outer façade was painted in the distinct Pompeian red and covered with black graffiti. It is from these notices that we know the owner of the caupona-and some of her barmaids. Aegle, Smyrna and Maria were probably of Greek, Syrian and Jewish origin. They may even have been slaves. But they were women with minds of their own for their names join that of their employer, Asellina's in their recommendations for the city elections.

~

"Hic habitat felicitas" (Here lies Happiness)

This is just some of the graffiti found daubed on the outer walls of Asellina's tavern. It could have been the recommendation of a satisfied customer-or perhaps an advert put up by the owner.

∼

As customers entered the tavern, they were greeted by a drawing of the god Mercury. Their arrival was announced by the unusual, phallic shaped door chime which also doubled as a lamp. The phallus was a symbol of good luck to the Romans, so this door chime may also have been a good luck charm for the tavern. Alternatively, it could have been an advertisement for the other services provided by the barmaids.

The caupona's counter was L shaped and inset with four large pottery *doliae,* which probably contained bar snacks of dried fruit, chickpeas or beans. One end extended across an entrance which opened onto the street where passers-by could purchase a snack cooked on a brazier at the back of the shop. The other end flanked the small inner room of the tavern so customers could purchase snacks to go with their drinks. Pottery lamps around the room would have made it smoky but atmospheric at night.

∼

A Typical Night Out?

The cartoons below were found in another of Pompeii's bars. They show the kind of activities patrons indulged in- and the pitfalls of a night out.

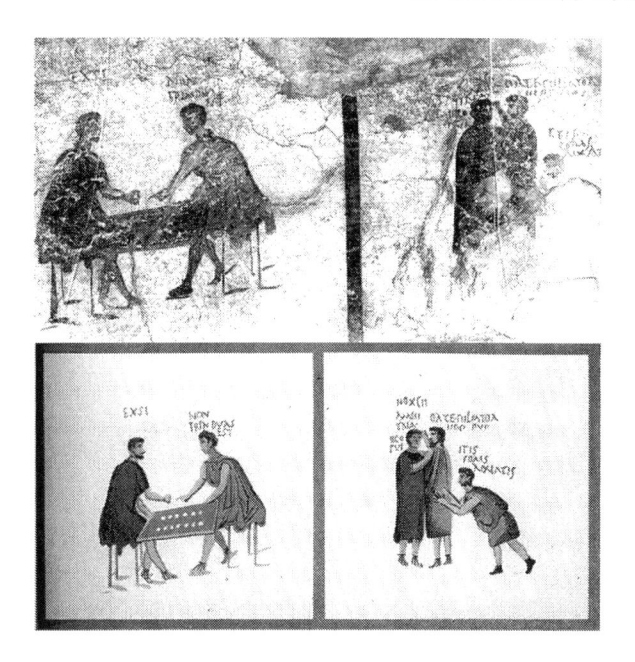

*The pictures (**Figure 61**) show two men playing a game of backgammon. "That's not a 3, it's a 2," says one man to his cheating companion.*

The pair then begin to trade insults and end up brawling. In the final picture, we see the landlord evicting the pair.
"Right, outside if you want to fight," he says as he pushes them out of his door.

∼

The patrons of taverns like Asellina's probably resided in the various rooms and apartments tucked above and behind shops, like the one belonging to Felix Pomatius across the road at I.8.1.

∼

26

ORDINARY APARTMENTS

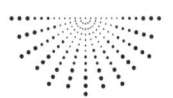

THE SHOP OF FELIX POMATIUS

Figure 62: Exterior of the Shop of Felix Pomatius

Rooms and apartments made up 40% of Pompeii's living space-many of them above or behind shops like this one on the right, the fruit shop of Felix Pomatius.

Shop fronts generally opened directly onto the street, fronted by a brightly painted counter advertising their wares. *Dolia;* large earthenware storage jars sunk into the counter, would have contained some of the goods for sale. When the shop was closed for business, a single wooden door would be pulled over the entrance and locked. The owner would then return to their living quarters. These were usually one or two rooms at the back of shop. They would have had some basic comforts: simple wall paintings and niches for the household shrine, perhaps basic toilet facilities and a cooking area.

Upper story apartments rented out from a landlord were often accessed by exterior stairways. The only luxury the occupants of these rooms might enjoy was a balcony. They would have made cramped family accommodation and heating and cooking on a brazier would have been hazardous.

Figure 63: Illustration of a Pompeii Street Scene, showing shops and the apartments above them.

The smallest of Pompeii's dwellings consisted of one room, squeezed between the other shops and houses, furnished with just a masonry bed. One such single room dwelling can be found in region I.II.37[1].

~

If apartment dwellers didn't want to risk cooking at home or couldn't afford a meal in a caupona, there was always the bakery. One example is just across the road at IX.12.6.

~

27

DAILY BREAD

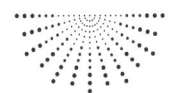

THE BAKERY OF THE CHASTE LOVERS

Figure 64: "Bread for Sale."

BREAD WAS POMPEII'S STAPLE FOOD. AS THE PICTURE SUGGESTS, IT was so vital that politicians distributed it to the electorate to secure votes. Roman bread came in different grades or qualities. The lowest grades were referred to as 'coarse bread' or 'bread for the slave'. But even homes with their own ovens did not usually bake bread themselves.

Types of Roman Bread.

Panis Siligineus *was the best quality Roman bread, followed by* ***Panis Cibarius, Panis Secundarius*** *and finally* ***Panis Plebeius****, which, as the name suggests was a coarse, common loaf. But the coarsest bread of all was the* ***Panis Rusticus****, which was made with bran alone.*

Basic bread dough was also enriched with wine, fat and honey to make a flavoured loaf and to vary texture. The Romans even had a pizza prototype: ***Panis Adipatus*** *that contained bacon- and bacon fat.*

At least 30 bakeries are known across Pompeii. Judging from the 85 carbonised loaves (similar to the loaf in the picture) found in one baker's oven, demand for bread was high. That made baking a profitable business. Many bakeries were basic retail outlets that simply baked and sold bread. Others were larger concerns with their own mills.

DISCOVERING POMPEII

Figure 65: A Carbonised Loaf of Bread

This building is known as the Bakery of the Chaste Lovers. It was one of the larger types of bakery known as a *pistrinum*, where flour was milled as well as bread baked. Dough was prepared in a room at the front of the building before being passed through a hatch into a back room with the oven. The milling room was at the very back of the property. Here, mules, whose remains were discovered in a stable on the premises, turned the mill.

Figure 66: Baker's oven from Pompeii

***

Did You Know?...

Pompeii's flour probably contained a good deal of grit from the mills. We know this because of the signs of wear and tear on the teeth of the town's inhabitants.

∼

The picture below shows what a Roman mill looked like. Grain was poured into the funnel shaped top stone, the *catillus* and ground between two stones in the basin or *meta*. Flour then collected in a tray called the *lamina*.

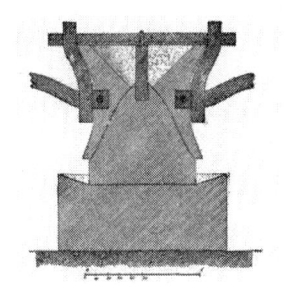

Figure 67: Diagram of a Roman Mill

∼

Roman Mechanisation

Mills were not the only 'machines' used in Roman bakeries. In one establishment owned by Popidius Priscus, archaeologists found an industrial scale dough-mixing machine. The dough was mixed using a series of large paddles.

Even kneading could be mechanised. Roman kneading machines wound dough around a horizontal shaft in a basin and then pressed it between wooden slats in the basin's sides.

∼

Murals were also found in the stables of the bakery, as well as in its large dining room, depicting lovers chastely kissing, hence the bakery's name. The wall paintings are relics of the days when the building was a house rather than a business. Perhaps the baker sacrificed his family home to the lure of profit.

∼

The neighbouring insula contains another family home, the House of Julius Polybius, found at IX.13.2-3.

∼

28
THE POMPEIAN FAMILIA

THE HOUSE OF JULIUS POLYBIUS.

Figure 68: Entrance to the House of Julius Polybius

FAMILY IN POMPEII AND THE REST OF THE ROMAN WORLD DID NOT just include blood relatives. Freedmen and even slaves were a part of the Roman *familia*, the group of people who formed a household which was headed by the *Pater Familias*.

In Roman society, the Pater Familias had absolute control over his slaves- and his children. A father had the right to sell his own offspring into slavery-even kill them. The only way for an adult

Roman male to achieve independence during his father's lifetime was for his father to formally 'Manumit' him, or release him from paternal authority.

~

The House of Julius Polybius

Figure 69: The House of Julius Polybius. A. Entrance 1, B. Entrance 2, C. Vestibule 1, D. Vestibule 2, E. Atrium, F. Cubiculum, G. Cubiculum, H. Reception Room, I. Reception Room, J. Peristyle and garden, K. Cubiculum, L. Cubiculum, M. Triclinium, N. master Suite, O. Oecus, P. Oecus.

The House of Julius Polybius started life as a lavish residence. However, by the time of the eruption of 79AD, it seems to have been in a state of flux. Much of its 700 m2 extent was either being renovated or had been downgraded.

The house consisted of two stories, centring upon the atrium and peristyle garden. Unusually, there were two entrances into the property from the Via dell'Abbondanza. These two entrances opened out into two essentially separate spaces which did not merge together until the garden area. It was here that the main, large rooms of the house were situated.

The front spaces of the house were in a state of confusion. Formerly lavish wall paintings in the atrium had been roughly plastered and the rooms seemed to be being used to either store equipment used in the house's renovations or else had been downgraded to an economic/industrial use.

Elsewhere, the house's expensive furnishings were found in odd, out of place locations, suggesting they were being moved around as redecoration occurred. It was in the garden area that most of the domestic activity seems to have been concentrated at the time of the eruption. Indeed it was here, in one of the vaulted rooms at the far end of the peristyle garden that the bodies of the house's last occupants took shelter and perished during the eruption.

∽

The Pater Familias of the House of Julius Polybius was one of two men. They were possibly brothers judging by the shared family name of 'Julius'. One candidate, Julius Polybius, was a local politician whose electoral notices have been found outside and inside the house. The other contender is Julius Phillipus whose signet ring was found in a chest in the building.

Whoever he was, Phillipus inspired proper *familia* sentiments in the servants of the house. A freedman, Cornelius Felix and a slave Vitalis inscribed the *lararium*-the household shrine shown in the picture-with a vow for his *'wellbeing, return and victory'.*

∽

A Close Familia in Life and Death

The Slaves of the House of Julius Polybius seemed to have felt a deep loyalty to their master. In two of the back rooms of the house (O and P on the plan), excavators found the bodies of thirteen members of the household, were they had taken refuge during Vesuvius's eruption.

The first room contained six adults-one of them a heavily pregnant female between the age of 16 and 18, adorned with jewellery. Lying next to her was a woman aged between 45 and 50, clutching a mirror, a bag of gold and silver coins. This woman was also decked out in gold earrings, bracelets and rings, which led excavators to identify her as the wife of the owner of the house and the young, pregnant woman as her daughter.

Near to the two ladies was the body of a young man, who was found slumped against a wall. In his hand was a small glass phial that contained poison. It is assumed he killed himself when it became clear there was no hope of escaping the eruption.

The rest of the family group lie in the other room, similarly identified by jewellery and valuables. However, in both rooms, were unadorned bodies of what must have been their personal slaves.

Slaves did not always stick with their masters during the eruption of 79AD, with many taking the chance to flee. The familia of Julius Polybius seems to have been closely bonded by ties of loyalty to stick together in life and death.

∽

Did You Know?...

Freedmen continued to owe allegiance to their old masters, even after they had been manumitted. If they did not show sufficient respect, it was possible for their former owner to re-enslave them

∾

Figure 70: Fresco of the Domestic Lararium

∾

Did You Know?....

Domestic Slaves were also part of the familia. It was common for them to join the family they served and take part in religious observances within the home.

In fact, masters and slaves could have close, affectionate relationships. One Roman master, Munatius Faustus, even included some of his slaves in his own memorial.

∾

The garden of Julius Polybius's house is shady and overgrown with fruit trees-just the sort of relaxed space you would expect at the centre of a family home. The House of the Orchard, over the road at I.9.5, gives some idea of Pompeii's other gardens.

∾

29
POMPEII'S GARDENS

THE HOUSE OF THE ORCHARD.

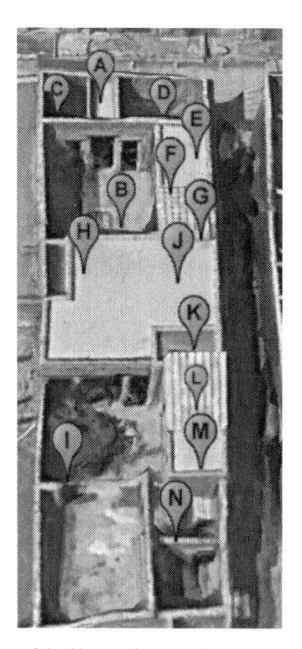

Figure 71: Plan of the House of Orchard. A. Fauces, B. Atrium, C. Stairs, D. Entrance to Shop, E. Room with water heater, F. Cubiculum with garden scenes, G. Ala, H. Tablinium, I. Garden, J. Triclinium, K. Cubiculum with garden plant frescos. L. Exedra, M. Cubiculum, N. Service Area.

EVERYONE IN POMPEII WOULD HAVE HAD SOME SORT OF SPACE FOR plants-even if it were only a window box or a small *hortus* or garden in a back yard. But the overgrown garden of Julius Polybius is unusual for a Pompeian townhouse. Although they often looked like artful wildernesses, gardens were usually carefully contrived. They were places to relax in. But whether viewed at a distance from the atrium or at closer quarters by a guest reclining in the triclinium, townhouse gardens were designed to act as visual talking points.

Figure 72: Garden Fresco from the House

These pictures of frescos, found in the House of the Orchard give some idea of how gardens were organised in Pompeii. Formal arrangements of plants drew the eye to carefully placed statues of the gods or other ornaments such as urns. Trellises or screens would have been used to edge plots or emphasise features.

Did You Know?...

Root cavities left behind by Pompeii's long dead garden plants and shrubs have been cast in plaster in the same way as some of the town's human remains, to allow archaeologists to identify some of the plants in the gardens of the town.

Figure 73: Second garden scene from the house

Carbonised remains of plants and root cavities tell us about the layout of gardens and the types of plants that grew in them. Symmetrical flowerbeds, edged with box and myrtle were filled with flowering plants such as narcissi, oleander and wildflowers. Fruit, citrus and bay trees were also popular, often edging the garden space. If the garden was large enough, plane, cyprus and acanthus trees could also be grown.

Popular Roman Garden Plants

A whole range of plants were cultivated in Roman gardens; some for ornamental purposes and others for health. They included:

Herbs: *Thyme, mint, savory, celery seed, basil, bay and hyssop.*

Flowers: *Roses, narcissi, oleanders, violets, crocus, lily, gladioli, iris, poppy, amaranth and wildflowers.*

Shrubs and Trees: *Ivy, acanthus, myrtle, box, yew, plane, and Cyprus.*

∽

The next stopping point is one insula along the road at III.2.1 at the House of Trebius Valens.

∽

30
GRAFFITI AND POLITICS

THE HOUSE OF TREBIUS VALENS

Figure 74: Entrance to the House of Trebius Valens

ELECTION POSTERS, SUCH AS THOSE USED BY JULIUS POLYBIUS AND Paquius Proculus were the usual way of mounting a political campaign in Pompeii. Elections were held annually for 2 *aediles* or junior magistrates and two *duumvirs* or senior magistrates (who were the pre Roman equivalent of consuls in that they were effectively the elected rulers of the city). Elections occurred in March with successful candidates taking up office on July 1st.

The exception to the rule was for the Quinquennial magistrate-the equivalent to the censor of Rome. It was this official's duty to revise the role of citizens. As his name suggests, he was elected every five years.

Over 2,800 examples of this 'electoral graffiti' survive in Pompeii. The slogans followed a set formula. They began by naming the person or group who commissioned the slogan (sometimes the politician himself), followed by the name of the candidate for election and the post he was standing for. Professional sign writers painted slogans at night. Some even autographed their notices.

Types of Election Slogan

Slogans designed to sway the Pompeii electorate can be found on walls all over the city. Each used various devices to persuade voters to support their candidates for office. These devices included:

Emphasising Good Character:
   "I beg you to elect Publius Furius Duumvir, a good man"

What's in it for you?
   "I beg you to elect Gaius Julius Polybius aedile. He brings good bread."
   "Marcus Casellius Marcellus, a good aedile and a great giver of games."

Finally, if in doubt, slur your opponent:
   "The little thieves ask for Vatia as aedile"

The house of Trebius Valens is a particularly rich source of information for electoral graffiti. The picture shows a sample of some of the electoral signs painted on the façade. One of these notices mentions a Lucius Satrius Valens. Alongside Valen's campaign poster is one announcing his intention of putting on games consisting of '20 pairs of gladiators'. This pairing of politics and the games was not unusual. Bread may have been the staple food of Pompeii but gladiators were part of its staple entertainment.

Figure 75: Election Graffiti from the facade of the House of Trebius Valens

The Layout of the House of Trebius Valens

The House of Trebius Valens was laid out as a standard atrium house. However, it had some unique and interesting features. Decorated in the third style, the house consisted of two stories. The stairs to the upper floor were in the south west corner of the atrium (B). Next to these stairs is a cubiculum identified as the master's bedroom (E). It was decorated in red and yellow decorative panels divided by the painted illusions of columns and was lit by a single small, high window. The name of Trebius Valens was scratched onto the wall.

The bedroom belonging to the mistress of the house has also been identified (F). This can be found on the east side of the atrium, with white walls decorated in second style.
When the house was excavated, a chest was found inside the room containing expensive pots of cosmetics-suggesting the occupant was the lady of the house.

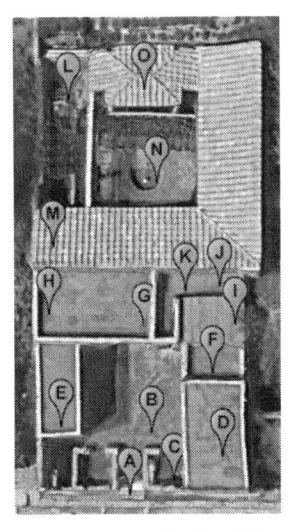

Figure 76: Layout of the House of Trebius Valens. A. Fauces, B. Atrium, C. Anteroom, D. Oecus, E. Master's cubiculum, F. Mistress's cubiculum, G. Tablinium, H. Triclinium, I. Service area with bath furnace, J. Tepidarium, K. Caldarium, L. kitchen, M. Posticum (tradesman's entrance, N. pool and Fountain, O. Summer Triclinium.

The House of Trebius Valens is also notable for having the smallest private bathhouse in Pompeii (J and K). Bath suites in private houses usually only ever consisted of two rooms: a tepidarium, which doubled as a changing room and a caldarium in which the actual bath was located. In the house of Trebius Valens, these rooms are both just 1.7 metres wide and no more than 2 metres long. The tepidarium led into the caldarium through a closed door. Both rooms were windowless and lit only by lamps to help retain the heat.

∽

The remains of a mysterious building two insula along the road at III.3.6 may also be linked to gladiators.

∽

31
GLADIATORS

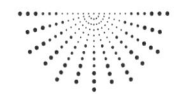

THE ARMATURARUM

Figure 77: Exterior of the Armaturarum (Before its collapse)

GLADIATORS WERE GENERALLY CRIMINALS OR SLAVES, ALTHOUGH some were free men who, out of desperation or a desire for money and fame signed up voluntarily for the arena. In such cases, a contract would be drawn up to determine the volunteer's length of service.

After an initial training period, the gladiator became a novice gladiator, a *Tiro*. This status ended as soon as he fought- and survived-his first fight. Then, the gladiator was classed as a veteran.

Gladiators were highly trained and well cared for and so a major investment for their schools. So it was not uncommon for losers to be reprieved especially if they had a good reputation as a fighter.

Types of Gladiators, their Armour and their Weapons

Thracian: *Curved sword, small shield and leg plates.*

Murmilliones: *Named after a salt-water fish, this fighter had a long shield, and the classic gladius sword.*

Hoplomachi: *Armed with a lance and short sword. Wore a Boetic helmet and defended with a small bronze shield.*

Retarii: *Wore no helmet, sword or leg armour. The Retarius's only protection was on the left shoulder. They were armed with a net and trident.*

Sectores/Contravetarii: *Similar to the murmillo but with a helmet.*

Provocatores: *rectangular shield, breastplates, leg plate on left leg only, fought with a shield and short sword.*

Essedarii: *Fought in a two-wheeled chariot.*

Equites: *Horsemen with lances and swords.*

Laquearius: *lasso*

Dimachaeri: *two swords.*

Velites: *spear.*

It was, however, rare for a gladiator to live a long life. Those who did win their freedom could retire. However with few options for a life outside the arena, many became freelancers or trainers.

Figure 78: The Interior of the Armaturarum

This building was known as the Armaturarum. Although it has now collapsed, the photograph shows what once remained here. Descriptions also exist of what it looked like when first excavated. Its pediment roof must have made it look like a small temple. But other features do not point to a religious function.

The wide opening of the Armaturarum was closed with a grill rather than a door. On the building's façade were frescos showing martial pursuits. The interior, shown in the photograph below, continued this military theme. The walls were painted with scenes of winged victories bearing shields and weapons. Interior cupboards may have held military style equipment. One theory suggests that the Armaturarum was a storehouse for the gladiator's equipment. Perhaps this was the case. The building is located very close to the amphitheatre district.

The House of the Gladiators

The House of the Gladiators is not included on this tour but can be found at V, 5.3). The building started life as a private residence but sometime in the early first century AD it became a training centre for gladiators.

Between 15-20 men lived in the house at any one time. They left hundreds of pieces of graffiti on the walls of the residence. This graffiti helps us to establish that chariot fighters, traex, murmillo, retarii, and eques were all popular types of fighters in Pompeii.

The graffiti also preserves the name of gladiators who were successful in the arena-and out of it!

Celadus was a gladiator who happily recorded he had won all of his three fights. However, it seems Celadus was a success out of the arena too. Various other scribblings around the house refer to him as 'a girl's heart throb' and 'the girl's idol."

Was this the truth or wishful thinking on Celadus's part?

We will never know.

∼

This area of Pompeii was also close to the countryside. The House of Octavius Quartius, two insula down the road at II.2.2 shows how rural life could provide inspiration within the town.

∼

32
A COUNTRY VILLA IN THE TOWN

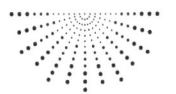

THE HOUSE OF OCTAVIUS QUARTIUS

Figure 79: View of part of the Garden

THE HOUSE OF LOREIUS TIBURTINUS OR OCTAVIUS QUARTIUS- THE man believed to be its last owner-was extensively remodelled after the earthquake of 62AD. The most obvious alteration was to the gardens.

The gardens are relocated to the back of the house and occupy most of the insula. As the plan shows, the house opened onto a terrace, which was shaded by pergolas and horizontally split by a miniature canal. Beyond this was a long landscaped area with a large, central bridged canal (L). This resembled the water features used in country villas to represent the River Nile. The canal ran the length of the garden, flanked by rows of statues and large trees.

Some believe Octavius Quartius was a 'new man' who reshaped his property to resemble a country house in order to appear aristocratic. Others believe the garden is simply innovative. There is also a further possibility. The use of miniature Niles could be a direct reference to Egypt rather than a Roman country house. One of the smaller canals terminates at a shrine to the Egyptian Goddess Isis. Perhaps the owner was a follower of her cult who wanted to show off his devotion to the goddess in his home.

DISCOVERING POMPEII

Figure 80: Plan of the House of Octavius Quartius. A. Fauces, B Atrium, C Ala, D Oecus, E Service area and latrines, F Small peristyle, G Small cubiculum, H Cubiculum, I Oecus, J Triclinium, K Garden, L Canal and pergola, M Biclinium, N Temple of Diana and Achteon, O Monumental Fountain.

∼

In the next insula at II.3.3, the House of the Marine Venus shows how those without the room for a villa style garden connected with the countryside in other ways.

∼

33
SMALL GARDENS

THE HOUSE OF THE MARINE VENUS

Figure 81: Fresco of Venus in a Shell.

IF SPACE WAS LIMITED, IT WAS POSSIBLE TO MAKE A PERISTYLE garden appear larger than it was and give it a rural aspect. In the House of the Marine Venus or Venus in a Shell, murals were used to create the illusion of more space. Features for which there was little room in the garden, such as trees, were incorporated into the pictures.

Figure 82: Layout of the House of Venus in a Shell. A. Entrance, B. Service Area, C. Atrium, D. triclinium, E. Living Room, F. Tablinium, G. Garden, H. Wall with the Fresco of Venus in a Shell, I. Peristyle, J. Cubiculum

∼

The Layout of the House of the Marine Venus

The House of the Marine Venus was initially excavated in the 1930s. It was damaged during the bombing of Pompeii during the Second World

War but in 1952, Amedeo Maiuri re-excavated and restored the building.

The service areas of the house, in the far northwest of the house had two separate street accesses situated just to the left of the main entrance. This area was connected to the main house by a single doorway in the far northwest corner of the atrium.

The main entrance of the House was flanked on either side by two cubicula. All three opened out onto a Tuscan style atrium (C). However, the house does not follow the typical atrium house pattern. While many of the leisure and dining areas were centred on the atrium, the tablinium or study (F), which usually followed the same visual axis of the fauces and atrium was instead tucked out of view on the eastern side of the peristyle.

These atrium centred leisure rooms were non the less impressive. On the northwestern side of the atrium is a barrel-vaulted triclinium, painted with frescos of balconies and peacocks (D). Next door to this is a much larger living room (E) that at the time of the eruption was still being redecorated.

Finally, the atrium opens out onto an **ambulacrum** or walkway, which surrounds the peristyle garden (G) on three sides. The rooms to the west of the garden open out onto the walkway while the two rooms just after the tablinium are hidden away behind a wall covered with the garden frescos. The walkway ended at the south end of the garden where a vast mural replaced rooms. This wall was the centrepiece of a vast illusion at play in the garden (H).

~

Figure 83: Fresco of Garden Features from the House of Venus in a Shell

Viewed from the atrium, the garden murals seemed to suggest the garden was part of a wider, rural landscape. The first picture with a fountain shows a painted wicker garden fence. Beyond this is a wilderness of trees, taking the house beyond the town into the countryside. The main scene which occupied the garden's southern wall created an illusion of the coastline beyond the house. In its centre was the image of Venus, reclining on a shell, which gives the house its name.

∼

Gardens, along with the other properties in the neighbouring insula at II.4. were up for rent in 79AD.

∼

34
A HIGH CLASS LEISURE CENTRE

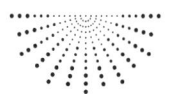

THE PROPERTIES OF JULIA FELIX

Figure 84: Still life with eggs, birds and bronze dishes from the House of Julia Felix

THE PROPERTIES OF JULIA FELIX WERE PART OF AN INTERCONNECTED high-class leisure complex. Composed of a house, baths and a series of eateries, it also seemed to have offered accommodation.

"To let" stated the rental notice found, still pinned to the property when the buildings were rediscovered, *"in the estate of Julia Felix, daughter of Spurius; elegant baths for respectable people, shops with other rooms and apartments. From the 13th August next until 13th*

August of the sixth year, for five continuous years. The lease will expire at the end of the five years." [1]

Figure 85: Layout of the properties of Julia Felix. THE HOUSE: A. Atrium, B. Service area, C. service corridor, D. Ambulatory, E. Central Garden, F. Summer Triclinium, G. Doorway to the second atrium, H. Second atrium, I. Biclinium, J. Tablinium. THE BATHS: K. Courtyard, L. Apodyterium, M. Tepidarium, N. Caldarium, O. Toilets, P. Open Air Pool. THE SHOPS: Q. Thermopolium, R. Dining Room.

The entrance to the bath complex (marked k-p on the plan) was from the Via dell' Abbondanza. Also fronting the properties was a restaurant (r) and a small-interconnected wine shop (q). Most customers of the restaurant dined seated in booths but private parties could rent a dining room that had couches set about a circular table. A little caupona offered a takeout service to the street and to the bathhouse patrons, who were served food and drink through a hatch in the wall dividing the two properties.

The baths themselves were linked to an elegant house (a-j) by a service corridor (b). At the centre of both these properties were the gardens. Perhaps people who wanted to relax after their bath or to take a meal in one of the outdoor dining rooms used them. This interconnection between house, gardens and bathhouse suggests they were once part of a private residence, turned into a business for profit or by necessity.

The baths in particular would have been popular with 'respectable' Pompeian residents without their own bath suites. In 79AD many of the public baths were undergoing repairs. The close proximity of the amphitheatre would also have ensured a flow of patrons. Julia Felix's complex would have provided a welcome break from the heat and excitement of the day's games, also offering discerning guests an upmarket place to relax, enjoy a bite to eat and a glass or two of wine.

∼

Some of this wine may have come from the property over the road at III.7.

35
VINTAGE POMPEII

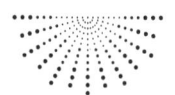

A POMPEIIAN WINERY AND VINEYARD.

Figure 86: A Pompeiian vineyard

INITIALLY, ROMAN WINE WAS NOT DRUNK WIDELY THROUGHOUT society. According to the laws of Romulus, only free men over the age of 35 were allowed to imbibe while women and slaves were completely forbidden. Ancient tradition stated that Roman husbands were entitled to kill their wives if they were found drinking. This led to the custom of husbands greeting their wives with a kiss when they returned home-to ensure they had not been indulging on the sly!

However, by the republic, these prohibitions were becoming relaxed and wine drinking had spread right across society. Wine was believed to have health benefits: to aid sleep and the digestive system.

Roman wine was usually never drunk neat. Older wines especially could be syrupy and very alcoholic. So it was usual to mix wine with water and to also add various condiments to it. Fruit, herbs and spices were commonly added to enhance flavour and colour, as Roman wines did not always keep well. Wine was also often served warm.

∼

There were are many types of Roman wine. Some were named according to their vintage, others according to how they were made and the ingredients used. They include:

Falernum: a white wine, drunk aged.

Calenum. A light white wine, favoured by patricians

Albanum. Either dry or sweet, this wine needed 15 years to mature

Massilitanium: a health wine, smoky and unpleasant tasting.

Mulsum: an aperitif, mixed with honey either during or after fermentation.

Passum. Raisin wine

Conditum. A wine mixed with pepper, honey and seawater

Lora: The wine of slaves, lora was made from the left over grape pulp

Posca: this vinegar based drink was popular with travellers as it was used to flavour and cleanse unreliable drinking water. It was often flavoured with spice and honey and was reputably refreshing. Posca was the drink given to Christ on the cross, showing serving him 'vinegar' was not the cruel gesture it was reputed to be.

Figure 87: Mosaic of Vineyard workers

Agricultural plots, like gardens were common in Pompeii. 10% of land was dedicated to small, market gardens growing fruit and vegetables or vineyards at the back of inns. This ½ hectare plot just off the Via dell Abbondanza was used to grow vines and some olive trees. Wine presses and large *dolia* show that it was also a winery capable of producing around 1000 litres.

This local vintage may have been exported elsewhere in Italy. Pompeian wines had quite a reputation for potency. Pliny the

Elder described them as *"injurious because of the hangover they cause which persists until noon the following day."* [1]

~

Popular Wines in Pompeii

Besides their homegrown vintages, the people of Pompeii enjoyed a variety of wines imported from elsewhere. Wine amphorae were usually labeled, showing the place of origin and the type of wine they contained. It is evidence like this that allows us to identify popular wines in Pompeii.

Many amphorae were inscribed in Greek, which is how we know wine from Crete was a popular import. Other foreign wines on sale in Pompeii included the vintages from Tauromenium in Sicily and the Sof wine of Cos.
However local Campanian wine was the most popular, such as the famous Falerian and Setian.

~

Perhaps some of those hangovers were acquired at the refreshment stalls erected in rented spaces around the exterior of Pompeii's arena.

~

36
SPECTACULA

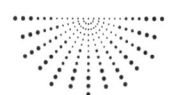

THE AMPHITHEATRE

Figure 88: Exterior of the Amphitheatre

'ARENAS' WERE NAMED AFTER THE GREEK FOR SAND. BUT THE Romans originally knew them by the Latin term, '*Spectacula*'. 'Amphitheatre', another Greek term, was applied to them later.

The Structure of Pompeii's Amphitheatre

The design of Pompeii's amphitheatre was very simple. It measured 135 metres long and 104 metres wide and its arena was sunk into a pit that was excavated 6 metres into the ground.

Earth from these diggings was heaped up into embankments that formed the basis of the seating area. Those seats closest to the arena would have been barely separated from the action below, with nothing but a 2-metre balustrade between their occupants and the fighting.

The south and east sides of the amphitheatre were contained by the city walls, with purpose built retaining walls added to the north and west. External staircases were built into these walls leading to the seating area. There were only two entrances to the arena: The Porta Triumphalis, which was used for the opening processions, and the Porta Libitinensis, which was the exit point for the dead.

Improvements were made after the earthquake of 62AD. New seating was constructed and buttresses were added to support the access tunnels. In addition, a covered walkway was added to the seating area to allow the city's elite to enter separately from the rest of the populace

~

Pompeii's Spectacula, which predates any stone arena in Rome, was built after the town became a roman colony in 70BC. It is also the oldest surviving Roman amphitheatre in the world.

~

Did You Know?...

The eruption in 79AD did not destroy the amphitheatre. Instead, it became buried under volcanic deposits. However, its uppermost parts remained partially exposed until the Middle Ages.

Figure 89: Dedicatory Inscription at the Amphitheatre

The dedicatory inscription, pictured above reads:

'Gaius Quinctius Valgus, son of Gaius and Marcus Portius, son of Marcus quinquennial duumvirs, for the honour of the colony, saw the construction of the amphitheatre at their own expense and gave the area to the colonists in perpetuity.'

The Pompeian's enthusiastically embraced the Roman games. Records of notable fights were graffitied on tombs, as in the picture below. Often, this graffiti gives us the names of the individual gladiators.

Marcus Attilius: A Free Volunteer

Figure 90: Graffiti of Marcus Attilius and Felix

The names of a number of gladiators from Pompeii and Herculaneum are known. Aside from the gladiator Celadus, other names can be found in the cartoons depicting the outcomes of fights which have been found scratched onto the tombs that lined the roads leading into and out of Pompeii. There is Princeps (the chief) and Hilarius (Merry). These single names are the stage names of otherwise anonymous slaves forced to fight in the arena. However, the name of one fighter stands out.

Marcus Attilius was a gladiator but his name shows us he was no slave. 'Marcus' was the praenomen of a free man and Attilius his gens or clan name. This means that Attilius entered the arena of his own free will; he had, in the word's of Livy, "put his life's blood up for sale." Sometimes rebellious aristocrats would enter the arena for a single bout, to show off or to shock. The emperor Commodus in particular was a keen amateur gladiator, fighting under the name Hercules the Hunter. However, for a free man to sign up to a ludus was quite a different matter.

Gladiators may have been the rock stars of the Roman people but they were also tainted with the stain of death. To fight as a volunteer, a free man was taking on that stain. So, when Marcus Attilius signed a contract with his ludus, he not only gave up the next few years of his life but also his honour-permanently. Attilius also gave up his freedom because for the period of the contract, the ludus essentially owned him. For a man to do give up so much, they had to be desperate for money, not fame.

The match cartoons tell us a great deal about Marcus Attilius the gladiator. We know that he won his very first fight in the arena, during games in Nola. The 'T' after his name on the graffiti stood for **Tiro**-a novice gladiator. Attilius's opponent was a seasoned veteran of the arena, Hilarious, who, the numerals show had fought 14 matches and won 12. However, on this occasion, the V for **Vicit** was awarded to Attilius. Hilarius instead had to settle for an M for **missus**, which means that even though he lost the match, he did not lose his life. It that had been the case, a 'P' for **Perrit** would have appeared after his name.

Attilius's next fight was against another veteran Felix who had won all his previous 12 fights. However, Felix's luck ran out when he encountered Attilius. He too is marked as a reprieved loser. So how could Attilius go from being an unseasoned novice to beating two veteran gladiators? Given his obvious skill with the sword, he was most likely an ex solider fallen upon hard times. Volunteers were often veterans who could not make a living in civilian life. They had no trade but blood, and the discipline and comradeship of a gladiator school was comforting, being very similar to that of the military life.

∽

The Pompeian's fanaticism for the games was so great it caused a riot in 59AD. The picture of the amphitheatre, from the House of the Brawl at the Amphitheatre, records the event. Tacitus in his 'Annals' XIV.17 describes how a dispute over gladiators between the Pompeians and visiting Nucerians disintegrated into violence.

The incident earned the Pompeians a ten-year ban on games, which was only lifted three years later because of the earthquake of 62AD. The arena was one of the first buildings rebuilt after that disaster-probably to raise the people's morale.

Figure 91: Fresco of the Riot at the Amphitheatre

Like the Via Dell Abbondanza, the arena was a vital part of the life of Pompeii.

PART III
POMPEII'S LAST DAYS

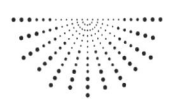

THE ERUPTION OF VESUVIUS IN 79AD

37
INTRODUCTION

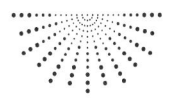

Figure 92: Vesuvius and the Ruins of Pompeii.

"A catastrophe which destroyed the loveliest regions of the earth, a fate shared by whole cities and their people" [1]

∽

POMPEII WAS ONE OF SEVERAL TOWNS OCCUPYING THE AREA KNOWN to the Greeks as the Phlegrean Fields-the area of Campania dominated by Mount Vesuvius. To the Romans of the early first century AD, Vesuvius was harmless. Its last eruption had occurred in the distant Bronze Age, making it, to them, a dead volcano. Vesuvius's 'burning' fields, enriched by the volcanic deposits of its eruptions were the only legacy of it's violent past.

In fact, Vesuvius was only sleeping. In 62AD, it stirred, causing an earthquake that devastated Pompeii and its near neighbours. Seventeen years later, the volcano woke up in a spectacular fashion. After nearly a day and a half of raining down ash and pumice on the area it had given life to, Vesuvius destroyed Pompeii. The preserved remains of the city and its citizens help tell the story of those final hours.

∽

The Tour

Figure 93: Pompeii's Last Day Tour Route.

A. The Forum
B. The Macellum
C. The Bakery of Modestus
D. The Via dell'Abbondanza

E. The House of the Ephebe
F. The House of Menander
G. The Triangular Forum
H. The House of Queen Caroline
I. The Forum
J. The House of the Golden Bracelet
K. The Herculaneum Gate and the Street of Tombs
L. The Villa of the Mysteries
M. The Villa of Diomedes
N. The House of Orpheus
O. The Street of the Skeletons
P. The House of the Painters at Work
Q. The Large Palestra
R. The Garden of the Fugitives
S. The Nucerian Gate

38
DATING THE ERUPTION

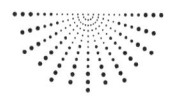

MOST PEOPLE ASSUME THAT THE FATAL ERUPTION THAT DESTROYED Pompeii was on the 24th-25th August 79AD. But while the year is certain, the month is not. For there is strong evidence that Vesuvius erupted not in the summer but in the autumn.

The Problem of the Ancient Texts

The eruption of Vesuvius, described in vivid detail by Pliny the Younger, marks the earliest datable volcanic eruption on record. Most modern translations of Pliny's work interpret the date given in his 'Letter to Tacitus' which describes the eruption as the 24th of August.

But this traditional date could be the result of a miscopying by scribes in the Middle Ages, according to Andrew Wallace–Hadrill, an expert on Pompeii. *"Principle manuscripts omit the month and a series of fifteenth century printed editions, which used manuscripts no longer surviving, give the month as November. Roman dates were often confused in the process of copying manuscripts so we cannot be sure of the 24th August date and there is a chance Pliny wrote 24 October. This version is supported by the histories of Cassius Dio, written a century later in Greek, who gives a long description of the eruption (Book 66, 21) and dates it 'kat auto to phthinoporon' i.e "at the end of autumn,"* Professor Wallace-Hadrill explained.[2]

Intriguingly, archaeology also supports the idea of an autumn eruption.

Figure 94: Fresco of Fruit from the Villa Oplontis, Campania

Botanical Evidence for an Autumn Eruption.

The organic wares found in the shops and warehouses in Pompeii, Herculaneum and Oplontis at the time of the eruption have been found to consist of freshly harvested autumn fruits such as pomegranates and walnuts as well as typical summer fruits such as dates, prunes and figs. These summer fruits had already been dried to preserve them over the winter. It also seems the grape harvest was already over and wine production was in full swing as sealed wine fermenting jars were found at the Villa Regina, Boscoreale[3].

The grape harvest would not have occurred until September and wine was generally in production for ten days before its burial for fermentation. All of this points to a post August eruption date.

Figure 95: Body cast from Pompeii. Note the sleeves which indicate the wearing of heavy clothing more appropriate to autumn than summer.

Braziers and Winter Clothes

Many of the body casts of Vesuvius's victims show that they were wearing layers of warmer clothing. Some have claimed that people put on heavier clothing to protect them from the eruption. However the presence of recently used braziers in houses such as the House of Menander suggests that the weather was much colder than we would expect in August.

. . .

Numanistics

A silver denarius minted by the Emperor Titus discovered in the House of the Golden Bracelet has added further fuel to the debate. The coin was found amongst the belongings of fugitives attempting to flee the town: a *"defined and documented context,"* according to Rosaria Ciardiello, a Roman archaeologist.

It is the reverse side of this coin that helps date it. Inscribed "TR PVIIII IMP XV COSVII PP", this describes the honours awarded to Titus: honours that offer evidence of the time frame.

"COSVII" refers to Titus's 7th consulship, which established the coin as 79AD. "TR PVIIII" refers to his 9th period of tribunical power, which was awarded in July of that year. However it is the remaining phrase of the inscription that holds the key. "IMP XV" refers to Titus's 15th imperial acclamation. In two letters dated the 7th and 8th September, 79AD, the emperor signs himself using the 14th imperial acclamation.

"This means that the eruption cannot have occurred before October 79," explained Dr Ciardiello[4].

39
SIGN AND PORTENTS

THE FORUM

Figure 96: The Forum

EVEN AFTER THE EARTHQUAKE OF 62AD, VESUVIUS DID NOT greatly concern the people of Pompeii. True, the volcano was only six miles away and the city was still troubled by damaging tremors. Here in the forum, many of the buildings were still under repair due to these minor quakes. It probably looked more like a building site than the heart of the city centre.

The Earthquake of 62AD: Decline or Renewal?

'I have just heard that Pompeii, the famous city in Campania has been laid low by an earthquake which has also disturbed all the adjacent districts...' [1]

On the 5th February 62AD, Pompeii was indeed 'laid low' by an earthquake which affected much of the region. Unknown to the local Campanians, the event was the first indication that the volcano Vesuvius was awakening from a long period of dormancy.

The violent tremors devastated Pompeii. Public buildings collapsed, the water supply was disrupted and homes damaged or destroyed.

Rebuilding began immediately. Seventeen years later, when Vesuvius finally erupted, it appears it was still ongoing. The forum was unfinished and many homes still being renovated and redecorated. Some experts believe this indicates that Pompeii struggled to recover from the earthquake. Others, however interpret the archaeology quite differently.

Pompeii in Decline?

After the earthquake, many of the grand residences of Pompeii seem to have changed from a domestic to commercial function. Some, like Stephanus's Fullery on the Via della Abbondanza completely converted the house space to accommodate a trade. Others remained in part domestic with the rest of the space given over to commerce.

When the forum was first excavated, many of the buildings such as the Capitolium were found to have not been repaired at all after the earthquake. Others were in an incomplete state, with marble facings missing. In addition, many of the statue pedestals in the forum were empty, suggesting that the statues had never been replaced.

The disarray in the forum could suggest that Pompeii did not have the resources to repair its civic centre. However, an alternative view of the forum has been suggested by John Dobbins, who attributes its state to post eruption looting. Once the ash had settled in 79AD, the tops of the forum's buildings would have acted as markers to those returning to the city to recover personal and civic valuables. Most of the statues and much of the missing marble facings could have been taken at this time.

Indeed, far from struggling to recover, it seems that Pompeii took advantage of the earthquake to modernise.

The New Central Baths

Whole areas of housing were damaged in the earthquake. In some parts of the city, these lost homes were not rebuilt. Instead, the land was used to build modern public facilities for Pompeii as a whole, such as it's first new set of public baths for just under a century.

The new Central Baths were spacious, light and airy due to their high vaulted ceilings and multiple windows. They were state of the art, employing the latest first century innovations in bath house technology. They demonstrate that there was no shortage of money for post-earthquake public construction in Pompeii.

Funding for Recovery

Some of the money for the restoration of Pompeii may well have come from Rome and the emperor himself. But other public works were funded in exactly the same way they had always been-from the pockets of politically astute local businessmen.

One such person was Numerius Popidius Ampliatus, a freedman of the Poppidii. As a former slave, he was barred from public office. But his son was not. So Ampliatus found a suitable project that would bolster his son's political career. The Cult of Isis was popular in Pompeii and its temple had been completely destroyed. After the earthquake, Ampliatus rebuilt it in luxurious style and recorded his generosity on the dedicatory inscription.

Ampliatus's generous gesture paid off. Despite being old six years old, his son was voted onto the city council as a gesture of gratitude.

A Warning from Vesuvius

The fact remains that much of Pompeii did resemble a building site in 79AD, with houses as well as the forum still undergoing repairs. But this activity was not a result of the 62AD earthquake.

Between the earthquake and 79AD, the seismic activity in the region of Vesuvius did not cease as the volcano slowly returned to life. In 64AD, a further earthquake destroyed the theatre at Naples during a visit from the Emperor Nero. Others no doubt occurred but remained unrecorded.

It was probably because of these ongoing quakes or tremors that much of Pompeii remained covered in scaffolding, right up until the moment of its final destruction.

∼

But life went on and the seismic disturbances became part of it. The picture shows Vesuvius as the Pompeian's saw it: part of the pastoral landscape.

Figure 97: Fresco of Vesuvius pre 79AD

But the summer of 79AD was full of signs and portents that warned of what was to come. The earth tremors increased[1]. The city's water supply began to fail as the earth subtly shifted, taking many bathhouses out of action. Wells began to dry up as the water table dropped. The frequent distant rumblings from the mountain would have seemed to the superstitious like the footsteps of invisible giants, woken from their sleep below the earth.

But these signs did little to prepare people for the events to come.

The next stopping point is on the right hand side of the forum at VII.9.7-8 at Pompeii's market, the macellum.

40
VESUVIUS AWAKES

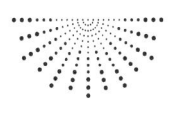

THE MACELLUM

Figure 98: Money lender booth built into the front of the Macellum

THE MORNING: 10AM-NOON.

Around midmorning, Vesuvius belched a small quantity of ash from its cone. This fell in a fine layer over villas and farms on its eastern slopes. The ash fall was accompanied by earth tremors. These were sufficiently alarming for the Lady Rectina at the Villa of the Papyrus in Herculaneum to summon her old friend Pliny the Elder from Misenum, to rescue the villa's famous library[1].

The people of Pompeii noticed nothing unusual. The earth had shaken before. And the small clouds gathering around the top of Vesuvius were probably not even remarked on.

Figure 99: Forum Scene, from a fresco in the House of Julia Felix

As the picture shows, the forum would have been packed with people buying, selling and going about their business. Shoppers in the *macellum* probably paid more attention to the fruit for sale, displayed in glass bowls, than the activity of the mountain that loomed over them.

Then at around lunchtime, Vesuvius literally blew its top.

∼

The next stopping point is the Bakery of Popidius Priscus, which can be found at VII.2.22 on the Vicolo del Panettiere. Leave the forum through the northern exit and cross the Via degli Augustalli onto the Via del Foro. Turn right onto the via Della Fortuna, then take the next right onto the Vicolo Storto. The bakery can be found on the left at the junction.

∼

41
THE UMBRELLA PINE

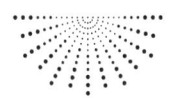

THE BAKERY OF POPIDIUS PRISCUS

Figure 100: Interior of the bakery of Popidius Priscus, showing oven and mill stones.

MIDDAY.

A violent crack caught people's attention. The earth lurched, throwing many to the ground. Vesuvius's cone had split from the sheer force of the eruption. A white column of pumice, speckled with ash and charred fragments of rock, rose rapidly from the ruined cone into the sky above Pompeii. This eruption column was formed from 22,000,000lbs of volcanic matter, forced out of the crater at a rate of 620 miles per hour — one-three times as fast as a high-speed train.

The column rose to 15 km, warming the air as it ascended. This caused the lighter fragments of material to float in the heated air, settling into *"a cloud of unusual size and appearance... like an umbrella pine"* according to the description of Pliny the Younger, who watched events from across the Bay of Naples. *"For it rose to a great height on a sort of trunk, and then split off into branches...Sometimes it looked white, sometimes blotched and dirty[2]."*

Figure 101: Image of Vesuvius and the eruption column

This fearful event would have prompted many people to leave Pompeii immediately. Across the city, remains of abandoned lunches have been found in dining rooms and kitchens. At the nearby bakery of Modestus (VII.I.36), the premises were abandoned with 80 loaves still baking in the ovens.

∾

The Bakery of Popidius Priscus

The bakery of Popidius Priscus was a Pistrinum-a bakery which milled its own flour — rather like the bakery of the Chaste Lovers on the Via dell'Abbondanza. Unlike the Chaste Lovers bakery, which was a converted private house, the bakery fronted a house behind it, the House of Popidius Priscus. This dwelling could well have been the owner's home as the two buildings were connected — hence the bakery's name.

Flour was milled using four large milestones and a smaller fifth one, all made of Roccamonfina lava. Just left of the entrance to the bakery was a separate, square oven room. The brick, wood-fired oven had a circular opening closed off by an iron door. To its right were supports for the wooden racks of bread waiting to be baked.

∾

Running now was a wise decision, for the eruption was about to introduce a new hazard.

Continue past the bakery down the Vicolo Storto, then turn left onto the Via degli Augustali. Follow up until the junction with the Via Stabiana. Turn right onto this road and follow it to the junction with the Via dell Abbondanza.

∾

42

A LETHAL RAINFALL

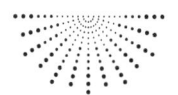

THE VIA DELL ABBONDANZA

Figure 102: Junction between the Via Stabiana and the Via dell Abbondanza

1.30PM

By 1.30pm, stratospheric winds whipped up by the eruption were driving the eruption cloud southeast towards Pompeii. It spread over the city. Sunlight faded and the early afternoon became like dusk. A sinister rainfall of rock and white pumice began. Pliny the Younger describes what his Uncle encountered as he drew close to the coast near Pompeii, at roughly this time:

186

> "Ashes were already falling, hotter and thicker as the ships drew near, followed by bits of pumice and blackened stones, charred and cracked by the flames." [1]

Some of the rocks or lithics were the size of an egg, some fist sized. As they hit the pavement and smashed roof tiles, people fled for shelter. Others risked the streets as they gambled on escape.

Figure 103: Volcanic Rock from Vesuvius

Lithics

Lithics are pieces of volcanic debris that vary between 15-30cm in diameter.

They formed just one part of the debris from the eruption. Other elements included ash, lapilli or 'little stones' which were less than 64mm in diameter and pumice.

A man assumed to be a priest, carrying only a linen bag of gold coins from the treasury of the Temple of Isis, may well have been one of those who risked the street at this time. He made it as far as the Via dell Abbondanza where he was knocked to the ground by one of these falling rocks. His gamble didn't pay off. The blow was probably fatal.

∽

Did You Know?..

High temperatures from volcanic eruptions can create pressure differences in the air. The air moves from high-pressure areas to low-pressure areas, creating winds. The greater the pressure difference, the stronger these volcanic winds will be.

∽

Elsewhere in the town, others placed life above their possessions. To reach the next stopping point at the House of the Ephebe at I.7.II, continue along the Via Dell Abbondanza for one insula. Turn right onto the Vicolo del Citharista and continue along it for two more insula. Then turn left, left again and then straight on at the next junction onto the Via di Castricio. The House is along the next road to the right, the Vicolo dell Efebo.

∽

43
HIDING TREASURE

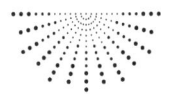

THE HOUSE OF THE EPHEBE

Figure 104: The Statue of the Ephebe

BY 2.30PM, ASH, PUMICE AND ROCK FRAGMENTS WERE FALLING steadily over Pompeii at a rate of five inches per hour[1]. Many of those indoors now had to make the decision whether to stay or leave their homes.

Options for evacuation were narrowing. Waterways around

Pompeii were now impassable. As Pliny the Elder discovered at around this time, the sea was becoming unnavigable as the eruption disrupted the tides. Like the River Sarno, it was also clogged with pumice.

But the roads were still relatively clear, even for wheeled vehicles. So some people began to gather what possessions they could transport and prepared to leave.

At the House of the Ephebe, the owner possessed a life sized bronze statue of a male Greek athlete or ephebe. The statue, which held candelabra in its hands, was used as a decorative garden light. Its owner must have prized it greatly. But as he made preparations to abandon his house, he must have realised he could not take the ephebe with him.

∼

The House of the Ephebe

The House of the Ephebe was large and luxurious. Occupying most of the east side of Insula VII, it was formed from three houses that were merged into one large house to cover an area of approximately 660m^2. The newly renovated house, was redecorated luxuriously in fourth style. This up to the minute decor, along with the house's stylish gardens and winter and summer triclinii showed off the wealth of the owner, P. Cornelius Tages.

Figure 105: Layout of the House of the Ephebe. A. Fauces, B. Atrium, C. Room with Stairs, D. Entrance to shop, E. Room with water heater, F. Cubiculum with garden scenes, G. Ala, H. Tablinium, I. Garden, J. triclinium, K. Cubiculum with garden plant frescos, L. Exedra, M. Cubiculum, N. Service Area

The main entrance can no longer be used to access the house as it was bricked up by the excavators. This is because inside a cast of the original house doors is displayed in situ, showing how they were firmly locked and bolted at the time of the eruption.

∼

Instead, the ephebe's owner removed the easily transported candelabra from the statue's hands and brought the ephebe into a room just off the garden (Room M on the plan) where it was carefully wrapped in cloths. Hoping that he had taken sufficient measures to protect his prized possession from the eruption, the owner of the ephebe then left, locking and bolting the door of his house behind him. Like many other Pompeian householders, he obviously expected to return.

But the possibility of leaving the city was diminishing with each hour, as people at the House of Menander soon discovered.

∼

The House of Menander at I.10.4 is our next stopping point. Retrace your steps along the Vicolo dell Efebo and the Via di Castricio. Now turn left onto the Vicolo di Paquius Proculus. At the end of this road, continue straight on until you reach the junction with the Vicolo del Citharista. Turn right onto the Vicolo del Menandro.

∼

44
HOPE FADES

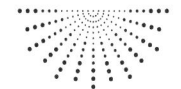

THE HOUSE OF MENANDER

Late Afternoon.

Figure 106: Fresco of the Poet Menander which gives the house its name.

By late afternoon, the people would have realised the eruption was not going to be over quickly. This realisation may have prompted many more to attempt a belated escape.

By now, Pompeii was a frightening place, in utter darkness. Pliny the Younger describes this darkness as absolute; more like a windowless, unlit room than the dark of night. The only hope of navigating the streets was to use lanterns like those in Figure 107 below, which have been found all over Pompeii.

All that was visible in the sky was the ash from the eruption, falling down like eerie grey snow. Half a metre of debris now lay on the streets of Pompeii and more was accumulating. Anyone travelling had to keep moving-or else risk being buried. Carts were now useless. The roads were only passable on foot.

The House of Menander was being renovated at the time of the eruption. The owner had moved out, but his staff remained. These slaves remained in the house until the end of the eruption, not even tempted to escape with the valuable household silver which was stored, along with money and jewellery in the house's cellar (R).

Figure 107: Lanterns found in Pompeii

DISCOVERING POMPEII

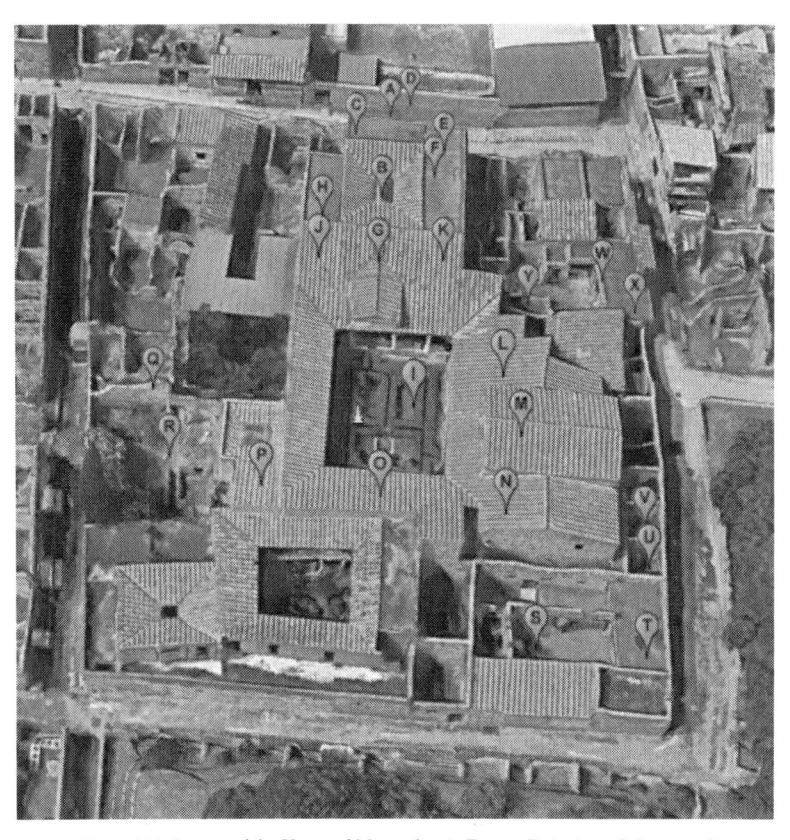

Figure 108: Layout of the House of Menander. A. Fauces, B. Atrium, C Stairs and Service area, D. Storeroom, E. Oecus, F. Ala, G. Tablinium, H. Cubiculum, I. Large Peristyle, J. Oecus, K. Triclinium, L Oecus, K. Triclinium, L.Oecus, M. Triclinium, N. Oecus, O. Central Niche containing painting of Menander, P. bath Suite, Q. Kitchen. R. Stairs to cellar and garden, S and T Stables and Slave quarters, U and V. Storerooms, W Back Entrance, X. Manager's cubiculum, Y. Service Yard

The House of Menander

The House of Menander was a high status townhouse, built in the third century BC as a basic atrium style residence. However, by the second century BC, modifications had begun and a new, fashionable Greek style peristyle garden was added to replace the hortus at the back. It was in a niche at the back of this peristyle garden that the fresco of the playwright Menander, which gives the house its name was found (O)

A seal, found on the premises suggests that by the first century AD, Quintus Poppaeus, a relative of the Empress Poppaea, owned the house. By now, a bathhouse with its own atrium (P) and entertainment suite had been added to the residence, as well as servant's quarters in the south east (S and T).

The architecture of the house was also being put to good use to express the wealth and status of the owner. Architectural features more usually found in public architecture were employed as decorative features to key exterior and interior entrances and focal points. There were even stone benches on the facade of the house which acted as seating for waiting clients. All of this left casual passersby as well as clients waiting in the atrium in no doubt as to the owner's importance.

However, the House of Menander also had an economic function. It was situated close to the countryside beyond Pompeii, and took full advantage of that closeness. Carts and tools were discovered in the stable yard of the house suggesting that it functioned in part at least, as an agricultural unit, as well as an elite townhouse.
This was not as unusual as you would imagine for Roman townhouses were centres of business as well as homes. The atrium and tablinium formed the owner's office area. Here, he would have met with his clients and conducted his business affairs. So it would have been perfectly normal for peripheral service areas-often with a separate entrance at the back of the house-to serve an economic function.

Besides being close to the countryside, the House of Menander was located in a hub of manufacturing and industry. Fullers, weavers and carpenters surrounded it and it is quite likely that the owner had an interest in these businesses. Their close physical proximity to his grand house would have emphasised the owners standing with his clients, not diminished it.

∼

Most of the slaves may have remained in the house but someone did take the horses belonging to a wagon already loaded with wine amphora, in the service area of the house. While the wagon was useless to them, the thief may have believed the horses could aid their escape.

However, by this time, there were other dangers on the street besides darkness and debris. Retrace your steps along the Vicolo del Menandro until you reach the Via Stabiana. Cross this road and head onto the Via del Tempio d'Isis and the entrance of the Triangular Forum.

∼

45
THE VIOLENCE ESCALATES

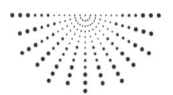

THE TRIANGULAR FORUM

Figure 109: Karl Briullov-The Last Day of Pompeii

EVENING

By the evening of the 24th, Vesuvius was ejecting 100, 0000 tons of material every second. Seismic shocks were shaking Pompeii with increasing violence[1]. Buildings and structures became unstable-as the picture above illustrates.

Two priests of Isis decided to leave the sanctuary of their temple with as much of its treasure as they could carry. Like their companion with the coins, they did not get very far. For some reason, they turned into the triangular forum. Perhaps they lost their way in the dark. Once there, falling columns crushed them, the treasure scattering uselessly around them.

Nor were those inside any safer from the tremors.

~

From the entrance to the triangular forum turn left. Turn left again at the next junction onto the Via del Teatri and then right onto the Vicolo dell Regina. The next stopping point is at VIII.3.14 at the corner of this road and the Vicolo dell 12 Dei.

~

46
NO REFUGE

THE HOUSE OF QUEEN CAROLINE

As day became true night, many roofs began to feel the strain of the ash fall. Hearing the creaks from above them, those hiding in buildings would have been wise to retreat into any strong vaulted rooms, underground suites or cellars in the hope of more secure accommodation.

But there were other dangers besides the ash fall. In Misenum, across the bay of Naples, Pliny the Younger describes how *"the shocks were so violent that everything felt as if it were not only shaken but overturned."* [1]

At the House of Queen Caroline two couples discovered the perils of hiding indoors. The columns and vaulting of the room they were hiding in gave way from the earth tremors. One pair was killed outright by the collapsing masonry. The other couple survived. They were able to reach each other through the debris and huddle together, waiting in the darkness as the earth continued to shake around them. But the fallen columns had trapped them. They died sometime later in each other's arms.

DISCOVERING POMPEII

Figure 110: Layout of the House of Queen Caroline. A Fauces, B Atrium, C Corinthian colonnade, D Stairs, E Tablinium, F Kitchen, G Cubicula, H Ala, I Lararium, J Passageway, K Second Entrance, L Triclinium, M service Area, N Stibadium.

The House of Queen Caroline

The House of Queen Caroline was discovered in the early 1800s. It was named in honour of Queen Caroline, wife of the Spanish King of Naples. Caroline and her husband were keen supporters of the excavation of Pompeii and often observed the excavations. This house was discovered in the Queen's presence.

The house was a typical high status residence, as can be seen from the *plan-except that the tablinium (E) did not open onto a garden. The Ala (H) opening onto the atrium (B), however was richly decorated with scenes of Perseus and Andromeda which were described as 'perfectly' preserved when the house was first excavated.*

Like the House of Epidius Rufus, the house is one of only four in Pompeii discovered with a Corinthian atrium. This unique feature was constructed from square columns set on a low wall which surrounded the impluvium (C). In the House of Queen Caroline, the columns of the atrium's colonnade were painted with foliage which made the columns appear to be surrounded by climbing plants.

A further unusual feature can be found in room L, at the back of the house, in an area which appears to have been a separate residence at one time. This room can be identified as a type of triclinium because of the presence of a semi circular dining couch called a **stibadium** *(N). The couch would have intimately seated three or four people, around a central circular table.*

∼

∼

Continue along the Via Regina, then turn up the Via delle Scuole until you reach the next stopping point at the south end of the forum.

∼

47
MIDNIGHT TERRORS

THE SOUTH END OF THE FORUM

Figure 111: Vesuvius, viewed from the far end of the forum

By midnight, the nature of the eruption was changing. At 33 km, the ash cloud had reached its peak. Now it began to collapse[1]. Sheets of fire and sparks of flames from Vesuvius punctuated the darkness.

Pliny the younger described these fires as they were at Stabiae four miles from Pompeii, based on the testimony of his Uncle's companions:

"Broad sheets of fire and leaping flames blazed out at several places,"

he said, of the scene as viewed from the villa of Pomponianus, where Pliny the Elder and his companions were trapped. *"Their bright glare emphasised by the darkness of the night."*[2]

In the early hours, Vesuvius released the first of six surges of superheated gas and light ash, which appeared as glowing red clouds on the flanks of the volcano. These pyroclastic surges, some of which reached temperatures in excess of 815 degrees Celsius, moved at speeds between 62 and 100 mph.[3]

Figure 112: William Marlow: Vesuvius erupting by night

Pyroclastic Surges

Pyroclastic surges are gaseous flows of ash and lava. Because they are composed of more gaseous than solid material, they travel quickly over large distances, often moving 10 km from their original source. Obstacles in the landscape whether natural or manmade cannot halt the progress of the surge and the speed and temperature of the gas cloud means that it is fatal to be caught in its path.

∼

The first two pyroclastic surges from Vesuvius destroyed the nearby towns of Herculaneum and Boscoreale where the people died from thermal shock. But they did not affect the southeastern side of the volcano.

Pompeii was safe. For now.

∼

Head north up the left hand side of the forum and exit onto the Via del Foro. At the junction with the Via delle Terme, turn left and then left again onto the Via Consolare. The next stopping point, the House of the Golden Bracelet is at VI.17.42

∼

48
THE EARLY HOURS OF THE MORNING

THE HOUSE OF THE GOLDEN BRACELET

Figure 113: Fresco from House of the Golden Bracelet.

2AM

By 2am, Pompeii was 2.8 metres deep in ash. The volcanic debris now reached the upper stories of many houses, pouring in through open doors and windows, filling atriums and gardens. Those within buildings with doors and shutters firmly closed, found themselves effectively sealed inside. Their only escape route was up: through the upper stories of their homes and onto the roofs.

In Stabiae, Pliny the Elder had already abandoned his room as rising levels of ash and pumice made him realise that soon he would be trapped. He joined his companions, who like the people remaining in Pompeii *"debated whether to stay indoors or take their chances in the open, for the buildings were now shaking with violent shocks and seemed to be swaying to and fro as if they were torn from their foundations."* [1]

With cushions tied to their heads with strips of cloth, Pliny and his companions decided to abandon their shelter. It seems many people in Pompeii began to do the same.

Did You know?..

Pliny the Elder was killed in the eruption of Vesuvius. However, the account left by his nephew helped preserve his name, for volcanic eruptions like that of Vesuvius; explosive, with huge vertical columns of ash are know today as Plinian Eruptions.

The House of the Golden Bracelet also known as the House of the Wedding of Alexander was one of the most unusual and beautiful houses in Pompeii.

The house occupies an area on the western edge of Pompeii

overlooking the city walls on one side and facing the Via Consolare. Here, the land was uneven and sloping which meant the House of the Golden Bracelet, like its neighbours had to adapt to the lie of the land.

And so it rose to the challenge-literally. The house stood three stories high-however it was its top story that opened onto the street. This meant that the layout of the house was reversed. So, the uppermost floor took on the role of the ground floor in a standard atrium house. It was laid out exactly as would be expected with a *fauces, atrium* and *tablinium*. However, whereas in a normal atrium house the *tablinium* would have offered a view of the peristyle and the private areas of the house, in the House of the Golden Bracelet these were on the lower levels.

A broad flight of stairs next to the *tablinium* took those with the privilege of access down to an area of entertainment and leisure. Here could be found the bath suite, as well as a series of reception and dining rooms, with windows that opened out to offer a view of the garden below. It was on this floor that archaeologists discovered the main dining room with its vaulted ceiling and mural of the wedding of Alexander the Great and Roxanne that gave the house its original name.

Figure 113: Fresco from Garden Room.

On the south side of this floor was a service area and a narrow flight of stairs that led down to the garden. Here, box hedged borders were eclipsed by the water features. A blue painted pool and fountain lay closest to the house, forming a focal point for the summer triclinium that had its own *nymphaeum* or small fountain in an apse at the back of the room. Water from this fountain ran down a series of steps into a channel that ran between the marble dining couches and out into the garden where it was piped into the central fountain.

The remains of the lavish meals enjoyed by the diners in the *triclinium* have been discovered by archaeologists. Fish, chicken, lamb and beef bones have been recovered, as well as those of pigs, partridges and shellfish.

The unusual layout of the house has provoked speculation that it was in fact a hotel and restaurant. During the early hours of the 25th, a wealthy couple and their two children were in residence. However, like Pliny's group, they no longer wished to stay. With escape from the lower levels impossible, the family headed for the stairs leading up from the garden to the upper floors. Unfortunately, they got no further.

∾

The Re-naming of the House.

Up until 1974, the House of the Golden Bracelet was known as The House of the Wedding of Alexander after murals adorning the dining room of the house.

Then, the remains of two children , a man and a woman were discovered near the ground floor stairs. Scattered around the bodies was jewellery and over 2000 gold and silver coins. The most striking find was on the body of the woman: a solid gold , double headed snake bracelet that weighed 1.33lb. The find overshadowed the murals. And so the house acquired a new name.

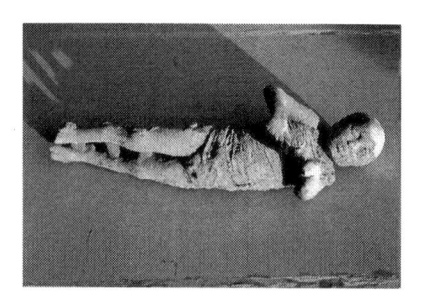

Figure 115: The cast of a small boy, part of the Family group discovered in the House of the Golden Bracelet.

∾

This family group became victims of the next phase of Vesuvius's assault on Pompeii.

∽

Continue north up the Via Consolare until you reach the next stopping point just beyond the Herculaneum Gate.

∽

49
THE THIRD SURGE PART I

THE HERCULANEUM GATE AND THE STREET OF TOMBS.

Figure 116: The Herculaneum gate taken from the Street of Tombs

6.30AM.

The victims in the House of the Golden Bracelet may have been trying to leave their refuge because of the lull in the ash fall, which occurred at about 2am on the 25th. They were not alone. Many others began to leave their hiding places in a last desperate attempt to escape Pompeii.

The only choice of escape now was by land. Aside from the fact the coast and the River Sarno were clogged with pumice and debris, the sea itself was in a dangerous state, with *"the waves ... wild and dangerous."* [1]

Those from beyond the city's northern walls would have made their way down this road, the Street of Tombs, hoping to pass through Pompeii to the southern roads away from Vesuvius.

∾

Figure 117: The Street of Tombs

The Herculaneum Gate and the Street of Tombs.

The Herculaneum Gate was the exit and entrance for traffic moving along the Via Consolare. It consists of a central archway for wheeled traffic and two narrower side arches for pedestrians. The gateway was built after the roman colonisation of Pompeii. However, around it are signs of Pompeii's early fortifications including its walls from the fifth century BC.

Beyond the gate ran the Street of Tombs. This area was just one of four Roman cemeteries in Pompeii. These cemeteries grew up around the roads just outside the town's Nola, Vesuvius, Nocera and Herculaneum Gates because of the Roman prohibition against the burial of the dead within city walls.

Despite their nominal separation from the living, these cemeteries were busy places. Relatives of the deceased would visit regularly. The Romans celebrated two major festivals dedicated to the dead, the Parentalia and the Lemuria when it was essential to visit family tombs to placate and remember the ancestral dead. Family would also visit tombs on the birthdays of the deceased. These visits were pleasant occasions. Far from being gloomy, the areas around the tomb were landscaped with trees and garden areas. Often families would bring a picnic which they would share with their ancestors through openings in the tombs. Along the Street of Tombs, there were also several rows of shops with residential quarters, showing some people had no scruples about living close to the dead.

The tombs were also a place to hang out, as the amount of graffiti found upon them shows, scrawled by fans of the games, or simply those who wanted to offload their problems or woes.

∼

Amongst the groups of desperate travellers making their way along the Street of Tombs at this time were a mother and her three children. At around 6.30am, they passed through the necropolis. The family appear to have wrapped themselves in layers of clothing to protect themselves from the remaining volcanic fallout. Even so, it must have been hard going. The mother held her youngest child whilst the other two children trudged behind her. Further ahead of the group was a solitary man who had just reached the Herculaneum Gate.

Although it was dawn, daylight had not returned. There was

also an unpleasant sulphurous smell in the air. At some point, the family would have heard a deafening surge of sound behind them. Perhaps they instinctively looked round to see what it was. It was too late. They died huddled alongside the tombs of the dead. The man just had enough time to shelter in a niche next to the gateway. It did him little good.

These two groups were amongst the victims of the third of Vesuvius's surges. This time, the gas cloud had reached the northern walls of Pompeii.

~

Thermal Shock

The temperatures of the pyroclastic surge in Pompeii have been estimated at between 250-300 degrees Celsius, based on the pale yellow colour of the bones of Pompeii's dead.

Death by thermal shock causes muscular stiffening that causes the muscles and tendons to contract, forming a pugilistic pose. Many of the bodies in Pompeii have been found contorted in this way.[2]

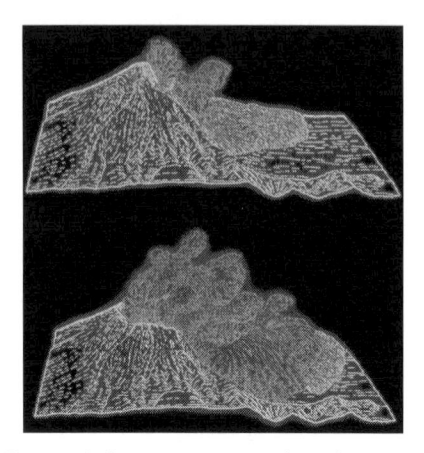

Figure 118: Computer animation of pyroclastic surge

Continue up the Street of Tombs onto the Via Superior to the next stopping point-the Villa of the Mysteries.

50
THE THIRD SURGE PART II.

THE VILLA OF THE MYSTERIES

Figure 119: Portion of the Frieze of the Dionysian Mysteries

Death from the third surge came to those hiding indoors, as well as on the streets. At the Villa of the Mysteries, a luxurious villa style farmhouse, the surge took all those inside by surprise. The doorkeeper died in his office, while upstairs three richly jewelled women were overcome in their rooms. Only a young girl seemed to be trying to leave the villa. She died at the entrance.

Did You Know?...

Of the approximately 1150 bodies discovered in Pompeii, 756 were victims of the final stage of the eruption.

The Layout of the Villa of the Mysteries.

The Villa of the Mysteries was first built in the second century BC as an elite country residence. The earliest part of the Villa centres on the Tuscan atrium, which was found decorated in the third style with Nile scenes. (O) This room remained the villa's main atrium throughout its life.

DISCOVERING POMPEII

Figure 120: Layout of the Villa of the Mysteries. A. Entrance, B. Service Area, C. Room with lararium, D. Corridor, E. Room containing Body, F. Latrine, G. Peristyle and garden, H. Torcularium, I. Second Kitchen, J. Main kitchen, K. Tetrastyle Atrium, L. Bath Suite, M. Cubiculum, N. Oecus, O. Main Atrium, P. Sacellum, Q. Cubiculum, R. Tablinium, S. Exedra with Veranda, T. Cubiculum, U. Triclinium with murals of the Mysteries, V. Portico, W. Wings of Portico, X. Viridania.

The original main entrance of the house was situated to the east of the atrium, where the house opened onto the Via Superiore, a road branching off from the Street of Tombs. A vestibule (A) was lined with masonry benches where clients waited to attend upon the master of the villa.

Between 150-100BC, the first extension of the villa was carried out. Now, a peristyle garden (G) was added to the east of the atrium. The villa's extent was enlarged by adding a buttressed cryptoporticus. A large terrace with a portico of limestone columns (V) was built on top of this underground passage.

This portico was later enclosed and two west facing wings (W) were added, terminating just before the western edge of the villa's tablinium (R). This room opened out onto the atrium in the usual way but instead of overlooking a peristyle garden, its western entrance gave way onto an exedra with three large windows, overlooking a semi circular veranda (S).

To the north of the peristyle was a small outdoor shrine or Sacellum (P), that may have been dedicated to the empress Livia. Her statue was found nearby just inside the peristyle, suggesting it may have been brought inside the house from the shrine to protect it.

To the south of the garden, a small bath suite was added (L). The baths consisted of a changing room or apodyterium, which opened onto a tepidarium. In the corner of this room was a small domed laconium: a hot, dry room customarily used for opening the pores before bathing.

The apodyterium of the baths also opened out onto a tetrastyle atrium (K). This small reception area with its brick built columns acted as a nexus point for a series of service passages within the house, leading to the main kitchens in the east (J). It was this kitchen that provided the heat for the bath suite.

The house had various cubicula or bedrooms at M, Q and T. These rooms are easily identified as such from the decorative bed niches built into the room. Some of these rooms seem to have been designed for multiple occupancy. Bedroom Q had a large niche, which could have accommodated a 'double bed' while room T had two bed alcoves. As married couples did generally sleep together, it is tempting to see room M as a master bedroom. It was also quite usual for bedchambers to open off onto an antechamber, such as bedroom M, which had its own oecus. Like room Q, this room also opened onto the peristyle.

The room containing the frieze from which the villa gains its name was used as a triclinium (U). The frieze, which stretches around the full extent of the room includes 29 life-sized figures, all playing their part in an initiation into what is believed to be either the mysteries of Dionysius or Orpheus.

After the earthquake of 62AD, the villa diminished in standing and became more of a glorified farmhouse than an elite country residence. More and more of the rooms were now given over to agricultural pursuits. The northern end of corridor D was the service area of the house. By the time of the eruption, this was also the location of a working wine press or torcularium (H).

The villa's last owners can be identified as the Istacidi family, from a seal ring discovered within the house.

∽

Those killed by the third surge died of thermal shock. The temperature of the surge and the ash within it would have caused fourth degree burns, which penetrated the muscles and deep body tissue without incinerating the flesh. This in turn would have overheated the blood to the heart and brain, resulting in death by cardiac or respiratory arrest.

∽

Even those below ground could not hope to escape this death. Move on back down the Via Superior to the Villa Diomedes.

∽

51
THE GREAT LEVELLER

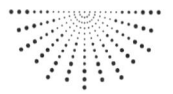

THE VILLA DIOMEDES

Figure 121: Street View of the Exterior of the Villa Diomedes

THE PICTURE AT THE END OF THIS SEGMENT SHOWS DEATH AS THE great leveller, dealing equally with rich and poor alike. This situation was vividly illustrated in the wine cellar of the Villa Diomedes. By the early hours of the morning of the 25th, it was the last refuge for 20 members of the household. Indoor and outdoor slaves, dressed in leggings and rough tunics crouched amongst the wine amphora along with their owners. The supposed mistress of the house sat nearby, comforting her young son with two young ladies, possibly her daughters.

DISCOVERING POMPEII

Figure 122: Layout of the villa Diomedes. A. Entrance, B. Peristyle, C. triangular Court with plunge pool, D. Apodyterium, E. Tepidarium, F. Caldarium, G. Kitchen, H. Anteroom to I, I. Cubiculum, J. Tablinium, K. Corridor, L. Terrace, M. Large Room, N. Winter Triclinium, O. Promenade with garden colonnade below, P. Belvederes, Q. Fish Pond, R. Summer Triclinium.

The Villa Diomedes

Named after the tomb of Marcus Arrius Diomedes just across the road from its entrance, the Villa Diomedes was another high status country villa.

The villa was constructed on two levels to accommodate the lie of the land. As usual, its public rooms were at the front. The entrance (A), a peristyle (B) and the tablinium (J) were all a metre higher than the street. However, the rear arrangement of the house, which included the garden area (O-R), was considerably lower.

Also found in this front section, next to the kitchen (G) was a substantial bath suite, which included not only a hot and warm room (E and F) but also a separate, changing area (D). The kitchen heated the bathhouse, with warm air flowing into the caldarium through the hollow walls and floor. The caldarium in its turn transmitted heat to the tepidarium through a hole in the wall.

The rear of the house consisted of a vast colonnaded garden (O) at the rear that was overlooked by bedrooms and triclinia (N and R). In the centre of this garden was a summer triclinium (R) sheltered within a pergola that overlooked an ornamental fishpond (Q).

~

The master and his steward were just outside when the surge hit. They had no time to take cover and the blast knocked them over, scattering the keys to the house and a substantial sum of money. But those in the cellar were equally as helpless. Some pulled their hoods up or tried to cover their faces. Two of the young boys died clinging to each other for comfort.

By 7.30am, the fourth surge was heading towards Pompeii. This time, the rest of the city did not escape.

Figure 123: Death and the Wheel of Fortune

~

Return to the Herculaneum Gate and travel back down the Via Consolare for one insula. Turn left onto the Vicolo di Mercurio. Continue until you reach the junction with the via del Vesuvio. Now turn right onto this road. The next point is on the right hand side at VI.14.20

~

52
THE FOURTH SURGE

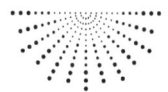

THE HOUSE OF ORPHEUS

Figure 124: Mosaic from the House of Orpheus

7.30-8AM

The fourth surge was the largest. Travelling at 62mph it reached Pompeii in minutes, breaching the city walls and covering the whole town with a hot, asphyxiating cloud[1].

At this house, the House of Orpheus, a guard dog remained chained alone in the atrium. He may have been left to guard the house or else had been abandoned by his fleeing owners. But the dog showed a tenacious determination to survive. As the pumice fall filled the atrium, he had climbed up the growing pile. But when the surge hit, his luck and his chain ran out. With nowhere else to go, he died struggling to escape his confines and the agony of the gases.

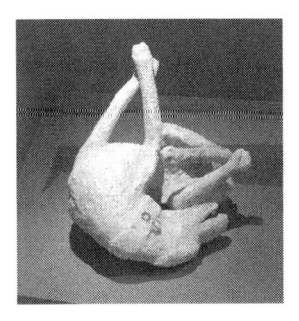

Figure 125: Cast of the dog from the House of Orpheus

Vesonius Primus and The House of Orpheus

The House of Orpheus took its name from the large but poor quality wall painting of Orpheus charming the animals, which adorned the house's peristyle (H). This tells several things about the house's owner: firstly, that he believed size was more important than quality and secondly that he had a less than refined background. Unlike many of the owners of houses in Pompeii, we also know the owner's name. He was called Vesonius Primus and he was a freedman and local businessman.

Figure 126: Plan of the House of Orpheus. A. Entrance, B. Atrium, C. Tablinium, D Passageway, E. Triclinium, F. Cubicula, G. Garden, H. Peristyle.

The name Vesonius Primus appears in various places about Pompeii from the period of Nero onwards. Primus appears as a witness on a wax tablet dated to 57AD and he owned a fullery on the Via Dell' Abbondanza. Graffiti on the wall of this building declared Primus's political interests. "Vesonius Primus asks for Cn. Helvius Sabinus, worthy of public office as aedile,"[2] reads the notice. However, despite being a local business man, Primus does not seem to have stood for office himself.

This was because Primus was a first generation freedman. His cognomen 'Primus' was not used by any of the other men of the clan Vesonius. The fact that it translates as 'The First' suggests that it was adopted by Primus himself once he was made free.

We know the House of Orpheus belonged to Primus because of a bronze herm and its accompanying inscription set up in the tablinium of the house (C). The bust was dedicated to Primus by one of his slaves, the cashier Anteros. The portrait is a realistic if unflattering portrayal of the master of the house. It shows Primus to be balding and wrinkled and was probably originally colourised judging by the traces of colour surviving around the eyes.

∼

Continue down the Via del Vesuvius onto the Via Stabiana. After two more insula, turn right onto the Via degli Augustali. Take the next left onto the Vicole del Lupanare for two more insula. The next stopping point, the Vicolo degli Scheletri is the second street on the right

∼

53
THE FOURTH SURGE, PART II

THE STREET OF SKELETONS

Figure 127: Skeletons

AT THE SAME TIME, A SMALL GROUP OF PEOPLE WERE MAKING THEIR way down this narrow street, which runs off from the forum. Like so many other people in Pompeii, the group was probably heading for the south of the city and the roads out of Pompeii. The man carried a key and had muffled his head with a cloak. A woman accompanied him, carrying her jewellery and more of the family treasures. Two girls followed them.

∼

The Street of Skeletons

On the 5th February 1863, workers of Giuseppe Fiorelli, the Director of Pompeii's excavations were digging in a small alley off the forum. They came across some hollow areas in the ash and noticed bones lying at the bottom. Rather than continue digging, they summoned Fiorelli who instructed the workers to fill the hollows with plaster, a technique he had previously used on hollows created by doors and furniture.

The plaster was left to harden and when the ash was chipped away, revealed the figures of four people, preserved at the moment of death.

These were the first human remains to be cast in Pompeii. They also led to the naming of the alley as The Street of Skeletons.

∼

When the surge hit, it knocked the group off their feet, blowing the older woman onto her back and her clothing up around her waist. The man fell, face down. One of the girls lay on her side as if in a foetal position.

This group was one of many found in this street which gave the street its name: Vicolo degli Scheletri or the Street of the Skeletons.

A few minutes later, a fifth surge hit Pompeii.

∼

Return to the Vicolo dei Lupanare and turn left onto the Via dell' Abbondanza. Continue along this street for 4 insula. The next stopping point, The House of the Painters, is just behind the House of the Chaste Lovers at IX.12.9

∼

54
THE FIFTH SURGE

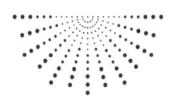

THE HOUSE OF THE PAINTERS AT WORK

Figure 128: Reconstruction of the House of the Painters in the Boboli Gardens, Florence

THE FIFTH SURGE WAS THE MOST POWERFUL. AT THIS HOUSE, THE House of the Painters at Work (IX.12.9), the owners of the house had the decorators in. The painters fled early in the eruption, leaving their scaffolding, paint and utensils behind. The force of the fifth surge blew over the walls they were painting completely intact. We know this because they lie over 2-3 metres of pumice that had already fallen over the course of the eruption. The force of the surge also blasted material through any openings, covering all the objects within with a fine layer of ash.

∾

The House of the Painters at Work

Although it is still being excavated, the House of the Painters at work has revealed some interesting features. The house acquired its name from the painters who were busy decorating the front oecus of the house.

The painters had only just sketched out the decorative design on the walls of the room when Vesuvius erupted- and the painters left in haste, abandoning their paints, tools and scaffolding behind.

Decorators and volcanos not withstanding, this irregularly shaped house was in a state of confusion at the time of the eruption due to the massive renovations occurring. However, unlike other residential properties after the earthquake of 62AD, it seems that the House of the Painters at work was still to remain a single townhouse. The type of decorative work and the presence of a large indoor garden or viridarium on the property suggest that it was intended to be a residence of some status.

∾

The next stopping point gives some idea of the sheer panic and despair of the last minutes of life in Pompeii.

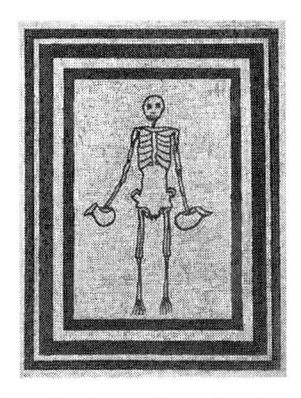

Figure 129: Image of Death from Pompeii

~

Turn left onto the Via dell Abbondanza and continue along this road for another five insula. Turn right down the Vicolo di Octavius Quartio, across the Via di Castricio to the road straight ahead. On the left is the entrance to the next stopping point, the large palestra.

~

55
THE FIFTH SURGE PART II

THE LARGE PALESTRA

Figure 130: The Large Palestra

MANY OF THOSE REMAINING IN THE CITY HAD GIVEN UP TRYING TO escape Pompeii. Instead, they sheltered where they could, waiting for what would happen next. Here at the large palestra, the bodies of around one hundred people were found sheltering under the portico that ran around the square exercise yard, which only a day earlier had been a place of life and activity. Many bodies were found pressed against the exterior of the door to the latrine, desperately trying to get inside.

The Large Palestra

Figure 131: Layout of the Large Palestra. A. Pool, B. Latrine, C. Entrances, D. Colonnade.

The large palestra was a public exercise ground next to the Amphitheatre. Built during the Augustan period, it was used to host sporting contests. The Emperor had acted as patron for these contests to encourage sporting prowess amongst the young men of Pompeii. A small shrine, possibly to Augustus has been found in the western part of the complex.

However, graffiti suggests that by the end of Pompeii, the palestra was used by more people than just athletes. The portico was the perfect place for teaching-as graffiti from a disgruntled schoolmaster who remained unpaid for his work indicates.

The palestra covered a square area measuring 142 by 107 metres.

Surrounded by a high wall on three sides, its south side backed onto the very edge of Pompeii. There were three main entrances, all facing the amphitheater, decorated with martial scenes that exemplified the athletic excellence originally aimed for within.

The edges of the palestra were marked by a shady, colonnaded portico that was slightly elevated from the central area. This colonnade consisted of thirty-five columns on the north and south sides and forty-eight on the west. Root cavities show that the edge of the portico was also edged by a double row of plane trees. Both trees and colonnade would have offered much needed shade to resting athletes.

In the centre of the exercise area was a public swimming pool, slanted to vary its depth. The shallow end measured 1 metre deep while the deep end was 2.60 metres.

~

The door of the latrine at the Large Palestra had been barred from within by another group of refugees. It is possible they had been sheltering there since the beginning of the eruption. One, an athlete, still carried his *strigil* and bottles of oil for a post exercise scrape down. Another was a doctor with his surgical instruments. They may have refused to open the door because they believed it kept them safe. If so they were unaware of what was to come.

But those outside were not. You would be forgiven for thinking that the man below had drawn himself up into this hunched position from despair. In fact, he was found in the large palaestra lying down. But his posture shows the effects the fifth surge had on those left alive in Pompeii.

Figure 132: A Victim from the Large Palestra

∼

Elsewhere, other groups had banded together in a last effort to escape. At the entrance to the palestra, head straight onto the Via della Palestra. Turn left onto the Vicolo del Fuggiaschi. The next stopping point is at I.21.6 on the right hand side.

∼

56

THE END OF POMPEII

THE GARDEN OF THE FUGITIVES

Figure 133: Casts of the Group found in the Garden of the Fugitives

IN THE FINAL MOMENTS OF POMPEII'S LIFE, A GROUP OF SEVEN adults and six children made their way in single file through a former vineyard, known as the Garden of the Fugitives. They may have already known each other or else met and grouped together as they headed for the road out of Pompeii to Nuceria

When they were hit by the surge that killed them, the man at the front, possibly a slave, toppled over onto his front, still holding the sack he was carrying. Behind him were two small boys, one holding a pot over his head. They died holding hands. A woman in the party dropped to her knees, seeming to press the fabric of her clothes to her face as if to protect herself from inhaling the ash. The final man in the group, however, does not seem to have died immediately. As can be seen in the final picture of his cast, he tried to struggle upright onto his right arm before succumbing to the inevitable.

~

Suffocation Versus Thermal Shock: How did the people of Pompeii die?

Around 1150 bodies have been recovered from Pompeii. Of these, 394 were victims of the early phase of the eruption, found buried beneath layers of pumice. Falling lithics-pumice and rock spewed from the eruption column-killed 10% of these early casualties, while the other 90% died in buildings when roofs and floors collapsed from the weight of ash and from seismic tremors.

But the other 756 were victims of the final stage of the eruption, when Vesuvius's collapsing eruption column released a series of pyroclastic surges-clouds of superheated gas and ash.

It is generally accepted that the victims of the surges suffocated. But recent studies of Pompeii's body casts suggests that the victims of the surges died a very different kind of death.

The Evidence for Suffocation.

The poses of the body casts have led to the theory that the victims of the pyroclastic surges were asphyxiated by the mix of hot gas and ashes. Casts such as the muleteer seem to be trying to cover their mouths and noses as if to protect themselves from the contents of the air around them.

According to the suffocation theory, the victims would have died an agonising death. With their first breath, they inhaled a mix of hot carbon dioxide, hydrogen sulphide, hydrogen chloride and sulphur dioxide ,which seared the respiratory system. These gases mixed with fine ash, which once inhaled, formed a kind of cement in the lungs. The second breath thickened this mixture and on the third breath , the wind pipe closed and death occurred.

The agony of this death seems to be captured by many of the casts. In the Garden of the Fugitives, a group of people were caught attempting to escape Pompeii in its dying moments by the fifth surge. One man seems to be trying to raise himself up as he was dying, while others are contorted into the 'pugilistic pose'

A 'Post Mortem Stance'

Anthropologist Pier Paolo Petrone disagrees with this interpretation. Dr Petrone has been involved in a close study of 93 well-preserved casts of the surge victims at Pompeii. He does not believe the pugilistic pose indicates the victims suffocated.

"The pugilistic attitude was erroneously thought to be the victim's attempt for self-defence." he told the author, *"This is exclusively a post-mortem stance. The typical body posture of a suffocated person is a floppy body, mostly standing in an unnatural position, just the opposite of the "life-like" stance of most of the victims found in Pompeii. "*[1]

Death by Thermal Shock.

Dr Petrone, is one of a growing number of experts who believe the bodies actually show signs of death by thermal shock. Dr Peter Baxter, of Cambridge University has also studied the casts from Pompeii as part of his work on the health aspects of volcanic eruptions. He described the effects of thermal shock in an interview with the author.

"The direct heat of the surge would be combined with the radiant heat of the ash particles in the cloud to cause rapid fourth degree burns, i.e., burns extending below the skin layer and into the muscles/deep tissues, with rapid overheating of the blood returning to the heart causing cardiac arrest and/or the brain causing respiratory arrest. "[2]

The Postures of the Pompeii Casts.

So what evidence do the body casts from Pompeii offer us of instant death by thermal shock?

The casts can be placed in two groups. One group display the primary postures assumed at the time of death and the other secondary, post mortem postures. Those falling into the primary category all seem to have been frozen in what ever activity they were involved at the moment they died. The post mortem postures are typified by the pugilistic pose.

Dr Petrone and his fellow experts believe the lifelike and often peaceful forms of the primary group of casts are caused by a condition called cadaveric shock.

"Such thermal shock induced an instantaneous muscular stiffening – known as cadaveric spasm – which caused the victims to be frozen in their postures at the time of the impact with the hot ash surge, "

explained Dr Petrone. *"The presence of this rare stance is indicative that people were alive at the time of posture arrest and its widespread occurrence is a key evidence that all victims groups were exposed to the same lethal conditions. The predominance of this feature in Pompeii victims points to an instant death due to heat exposure."*[3]

Death by cadaveric shock prevents the normal relaxation of the body after death-which explains why the victims of Pompeii maintained their body posture.

The post mortem 'pugilistic pose' is also taken as an indicator of death by thermal shock. Its characteristic 'clawing' pose where the victim seems to be struggling against death is in fact caused by the tendons and muscles of the limbs contracting after death due to the extreme heat.

"The burnt muscles contract – shorten as they coagulate – and limbs bend into a position which can't be straightened even after death, " explained Dr Baxter[4].

But why the difference between the two sets of poses? It seems that those sheltering at the time of the surge were more likely to assume a primary pose while the pugilistic pose was common amongst those caught out in the open. *"If the temperature was much higher and all the people were caught in the open then all the bodies would show the same attitude, especially as clothing would ignite in all of the victims."* Dr Baxter said.

But both postures have been identified by Giuseppe Mastrolorenzo, a volcanologist at the Vesuvius Observatory as typified by the victims of nuclear explosions-or volcanic eruptions.

Determining the Temperatures of Pompeii's Surges.

The thermal threshold for human survival has been determined as 200 Degrees Celsius. Dr Mastrolorenzo, Dr Petrone and their colleagues have been able to prove that the surges in Pompeii exceeded this level and so were hot enough to kill.

They heated batches of human and horse bones to between 100-800 Degrees Celsius – temperatures compatible with those of the surges emitted by Vesuvius. Burnt bones assume different colours dependent on the heat they were subjected to. The bones of Pompeii's victims were burnt to a pale yellow. This was the colour of the modern bones heated to temperatures of between 250-300 degrees Celsius.

Hot Enough to Kill-But Not Destroy.

In an experiment shown in a 2013 BBC programme 'Pompeii: The Mystery of the People Frozen in Time', a team from the University of Edinburgh replicated the effects of a pyroclastic surge in Pompeii. They took a piece of pork wrapped in a woollen fabric and exposed it to intense infra red radiation of between 200-250 Degrees Celsius for 150 seconds.

The cloth was left slightly charred but intact and the pork heated but otherwise unchanged. This established that the temperatures in Pompeii were hot enough to kill but they would not have destroyed clothing and soft tissues-which explains why many of the casts show the bodies retaining their forms, clothes, even hairstyles at death.

Thermal Shock Versus Suffocation.

The evidence for thermal shock as the cause of death in Pompeii seems unequivocal. But Dr Baxter does not rule out the part played by asphyxiation.

"At Mount St Helens in 1980 people were in the open and the surge was fast moving. Ash was forced into the mouths and lungs - bad news. When the windpipe is blocked you can't breath by definition," he explained. *" In a dilute, slow moving surge if the temperature is low enough you might survive the burns but still eventually die in hospital from lung injury due to burns to the lung tissue from inhaling hot ash. Either heat or suffocation gets you first in the surge itself."*[5]

Figure 134: The Last Fugitive

Nothing in Pompeii would have survived the fifth surge. For the city, it was the end. Pliny the Younger , witnessing events from Misenum, described how *"a fearful black cloud was rent by forked and quivering bursts of flame and parted to reveal great tongues of fire, like flashes of lightning. "*

The cloud then *"sank down to earth and covered the sea, hid(ing) the promontory of Misenum from site"* [6]

But the eruption had not yet finished. A six and final surge followed, reaching as far south as Stabiae and over the bay of Naples:

"A dense black cloud was coming up behind us," Pliny the Younger recalled, *"spreading over the earth like a flood."*[7]

The cloud narrowly missed Misenum but it gave the people there a taste of what their near neighbours had experienced. By the 26th, a pallid form of daylight had returned to the Bay of Naples. Pliny the Younger describes the scene in Misenum. It must have been very similar in Pompeii:

"At last, the darkness thinned and dispersed into smoke or cloud, then there was genuine daylight and the sun actually shone out, but yellowish as it is during an eclipse.....everything (was) changed, buried deep in ashes, like snowdrifts."[8]

In Pompeii, beneath the ash, the dead town waited.

∼

Return up the Vicolo del Fuggiaschi, turn right onto the Via della Palestra, and then right again onto the Via di Nocera. Head down the road to the Nucerian Gate and the last stop of this journey.

∼

57
THE NUCERIAN GATE

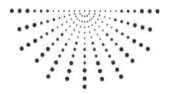

EPILOGUE: THE PEOPLE OF POMPEII

Figure 135: Vesuvius from the Ruins of Pompeii

AROUND 1150 OF THOSE WHO DIED IN VESUVIUS'S ERUPTION HAVE been recovered from in and around Pompeii. Those who had died before the pyroclastic surges were buried in the pumice layer where they slowly decayed, leaving only their skeleton. But the bodies of those killed during the surges suffered a different fate.

Casting Human Remains

Only 100 of the 1150 bodies found in and around Pompeii have been cast. The process of casting is by no means simple. Plaster has to be mixed to an exact consistency; thick enough to support the skeletal frame but not so thick it obliterates the fine details of the cast. It then needs to be carefully poured as the bones are very brittle and the plaster could damage them.

∽

Each surge covered the bodies with a layer of fine ash. This mixed with rain that fell after the eruption. The resulting mixture hardened into a cement shell. As the picture shows, the flesh inside the shell decayed, but the skeleton remained intact-as did an impression of the body at the moment of death. Plaster poured inside the resulting cavity produced a cast of the individual.

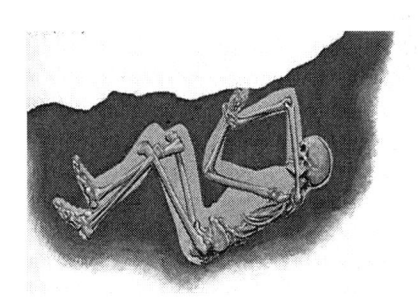

Figure 136: Diagram showing how ash preserved the body shape of the victims

Here at the Nucerian gate is another necropolis of Pompeii. Amongst those buried in tombs are the bodies of those who escaped the city in its final minutes.

The Nucerian Gate Cemetery

The cemetery at the Porta Nuceria is one of the most significant in Pompeii for it is the last resting place not only of the victims of Vesuvius but also the many of Pompeii's late and great citizens from the late republic onwards.

Amongst the tombs is that of Eumachia, businesswoman and civic patron. The tomb, which was one of the largest was entirely paid for by Eumachia herself and decorated with an Amazonian frieze-perhaps to emphasis Eumachia's independence and self-reliance. The large tomb was set off the road and surrounded by a wall with its' only entrance through a gate.

The cemetery was also the site of the tomb of Veia Barchilla, a member of an important Pompeian dynasty and her husband Numerius Agrestinus Egnastius Puchrus of the Egnatii. The dedicatory inscription on the tomb placed Veia first, suggesting that despite her sex, her family connections gave her the greater precedence. Her tomb, rather than being shaped like a house or temple like many of the tombs was a tumulus tomb. It was a masonry drum placed on a podium which was finished off on top with a mound of earth that would have been planted with flowers or herbs.

Then there is the twin tomb of Aulus Veius Faustus and his brother Gaius Munatius Faustus, a freedman and Augustali who built the tomb for himself and his wife Naevoleia Tyche. However, after his death, Tyche built a much more elaborate tomb outside the Herculaneum gate.

This tomb was dedicated by Tyche to her husband, celebrating his achievements in the Pompeian community and the honours the city bestowed upon him. The tomb records how Pompeii honoured Faustus with a double seat in the theatre. However, it also celebrates Tyche's *achievements as a freedwoman. One of the tomb friezes showing a larger than life figure of the lady herself on a ship-no doubt representing her involvement in trade. The whole tomb epitomises one of a Roman burial places primary functions: to 'immortalise' the memory of the deceased as well as house their remains.*

∼

Here at the Nucerian gate, the remains of the unburied dead of Pompeii reveal how they looked at the moment of their deaths. We can see their clothes, their hair styles, their facial expressions, and the spasms of their deaths. The casts preserve the humanity of the dead. They become people we can relate to, not as artefacts.

In fact, it is the people of Pompeii that make this city unique amongst ancient sites. They tell the human story behind the streets and buildings. They remind us that Pompeii, for all its wonders and fascination is much more than an archaeological site. Ultimately, it is the site of a human tragedy.

Figure 137: Victims at the Nucerian Gate

BEFORE YOU GO...

Did you like this book?
Please leave a review on Amazon.co.uk or Amazon.com.

∼

"Discovering Herculaneum" due out in 2019

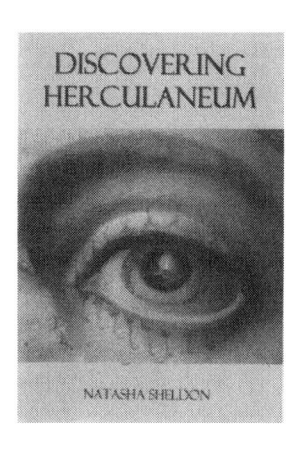

For more information, visit **Strigidae Press** https://www.facebook.com/StrigidaePress/

PICTURE CREDITS

∼

Unless otherwise stated, all maps and photographs are the work of Natasha Sheldon.

∼

Figure 1: **Tour Map for "Civic Pompeii"**
Figure 2: **Layout of the Triangular Forum and Theatre District**
Figure 3: **Reproduction of Doric temple and Triangular forum from the south** by *Carl Weichardt. Source: Mau and Kelsey's 'Pompeii: Its Life and Art'. Permission: Public Domain (copyright expired)*
Figure 4: **Hercules fighting Green (on the far right); Eurytion lays wounded at their feet; Athena (on the left) watches the scene.** *Attic white-ground black-figure lekythos. Photograph by Marie-Lan Nguyen. Permission: Creative Commons Attribution 2.5 Generic (c/o Wikimedia)*
Figure 5: **Bas-relief of Minerva.** *Photograph by Ken Thomas. Permission: Public Domain c/o Wikimedia.*
Figure 6: **The Quadroporticus from the stairs**

PICTURE CREDITS

Figure 7: **Computer reconstruction of Hellenistic theatre and triangular forum.** *Created by PublicVR. Permission: Jeffrey Jacobson, Ph.D. http://publicvr.org*
Figure 8: **The Monumental Gateway**
Figure 9: **Computer Reconstruction of The Monumental Gateway.** *Created by PublicVR. Permission: Jeffrey Jacobson, Ph.D. http://publicvr.org*
Figure 10: **Intersection between the Via del Teatri and Via dell Abbondanza**
Figure 11: **Overview of the Forum**
Figure 12: **Mosaic of Garum Amphorae from the House of Aulus Umbrious Scarus.** *Picture Credit: Claus Ableiter. Wikimedia Commons.*
Figure 13: **The Basilica today**
Figure 14: **Reconstruction of the Exterior of the Basilica.** Source: *Mau and Kelsey's 'Pompeii: Its Life and Art'. Permission: Public Domain (copyright expired)*
Figure 15: **Layout of the Basilica.**
Figure 16: **Layout of the Temple of Venus.**
Figure 17: **Venus watching over Aeneas.** *Source: Wikimedia Commons.*
Permission: public domain (copyright expired)
Figure 18: **The Temple of Apollo.** *Source: Mau and Kelsey's 'Pompeii: Its Life and Art'. Permission: Public Domain (copyright expired, pre 1923)*
Figure 19: **Overview of the Temple of Apollo.**
Figure 20: **Statue of Apollo facing the cella of the temple**
Figure 21: **Photograph of the Capitolium Today.**
Figure 22: **Layout of the Capitolium**
Figure 23: **Entrance to men's section of the Forum Baths**
Figure 24: **Plan of the Forum baths**
Figure 25: **Décor in the Tepidarium**
Figure 26: **Roman hypocaust.** *Source Ad Meskens/Wikimedia commons*

PICTURE CREDITS

Figure 27: **The remains of the Temple of Augustan Fortune**
Figure 28: **Roman relief showing Priestess sacrificing accompanied by a slave**. (Priestess (?), cult container put on a three-foot support, censer and sacrificing man, and small slave with can and bowl).*Permission: Public Domain by permission of Bibi Saint-Pol c/o Wikimedia*
Figure 29: **Centre of the Augustan Forum with exposed travertine marble slabs**
Figure 30: **Layout of the Macellum**
Figure 31: **Reconstruction of the Macellum.** *Source: Mau and Kelsey's 'Pompeii: Its Life and Art'. Permission: Public Domain (copyright expired, pre 1923).*
Figure 32: **Layout of the Temple of the Public Lares.**
Figure 33: **Layout of the Temple of Vespasian**
Figure 34: **Entrance to the Eumachia Building**
Figure 35: **Statue of Eumachia.** *World archaeology.com*
Figure 36: **Layout of the Eumachia Building**
Figure 37: **Reconstruction of the Temple of Isis**. *Original Creator: PublicVR. Permission: Jeffrey Jacobson, Ph.D. http://publicvr.org.*
Figure 38: **Reconstruction of the Purgatorium**. *Original Creator: PublicVR. Permission: Jeffrey Jacobson, Ph.D. http://publicvr.org.*
Figure 39: **Route of "Daily Life in Pompeii" Tour.**
Figure 40: **Fountain of Abundance, Via dell Abbondanza**
Figure 41: **Pompeii's Main Roads**
Figure 42: **Plan of Stabian Baths.**
Figure 43: **Photograph of the Water Tower.**
Figure 44: **Close up of fountain from the House of the Small Fountain, Pompeii.** *Picture credit: WKnight (c/o Wikimedia Creative Commons attribution Share Alike 3.0)*
Figure 45: **Photograph of Street front of the House of Epidius Rufus.**
Figure 46: **Reconstruction of the House of Epidius Rufus** *from Mau and Kelsey's Pompeii its Life and Art (1907) (In the public domain- copyright expired)*

PICTURE CREDITS

Figure 47: **Layout of the House of Epidius Rufus.**
Figure 48: **Photograph of Stephanus's Fullery.**
Figure 49: **The Converted** *Impluvium*
Figures 50 and 51: **Workers Putting up clothes for drying and whitening cloth (frescos from the fullery of Veranius Hypsaeus).** *Photographs by Wolfgang Rieger (c/o Wikimedia commons- In Public domain).*
Figure 52: **Lararium.** *Source Carole Raddato/Wikimedia Commons.*
Figure 53: **Fresco of Mercury leaving the temple** *(postcard, c/o Wikimedia commons. Copyright expired)*
Figure 54: **Venus Pompeiana.** *Picture Credit Filippo Coarelli (c/o Wikimedia commons. In the public domain)*
Figure 55: **Old photo c. 1914 of the Cryptoporticus.** *Public Domain*
Figure 56 and 57: **Plans of the House of the Cryptoporticus.** *Picture Credit: Peter Clements (Source: 79AD website. Reproduced with author's permission)*
Figure 58: Atrium of the House of Paquius Proculus. Picture Credit: Google Images
Figure 59: **Layout of the House of Paquius Proculus**
Figure 60: **Photograph of the frontage of Asellina's Tavern.**
Figure 61: **Murals from a Pompeii bar showing gambling and a fight.** *Photograph by Fer.filol. (c/o Wikimedia commons. Released into public domain by photographer.)*
Figure 62: **Photograph of the shop of Felix Pomatius.**
Figure 63: **Pompeii Street Scene and Apartments** *(c/o Karenswhimsy.com-picture in public domain as pre 1923)*
Figure 64: **Bread for sale, Fresco from the House of Julia Felix** *(c/o Wikimedia Commons. In the Public Domain.)*
Figure 65: **Photograph of carbonised loaf of bread, Pompeii.** *Photograph by Beatrice. (c/o Wikimedia commons, In the public domain)*
Figure 66: **Baker's Oven from Pompeii.** *Public domain image*
Figure 67: **Diagram of a Mill** *(c/o Clip Art. In the public domain- copyright expired)*

PICTURE CREDITS

Figure 68: **Photograph of the front of the House of Julius Polybius.**
Figure 69: **Layout of the House of Julius Polybius**
Figure 70: **Lararium from the House of Julius Polybius.** *Photograph by Wolfgang Reiger. (c/o Wikimedia commons. Released into public domain by author.)*
Figure 71: **Plan of the House of the Orchard.**
Figures 72 and 73: **Garden frescos, both from the House of the Orchard.** *(c/o Wikimedia Commons. Released under GNU Free documentation License.)*
Figure 74: **Photograph of the entrance to the House of Trebius Valens.**
Figure 75: **Election Graffiti from the Wall of the House of Trebius Valens.** *(Source: Postcard, c/o Wikimedia Commons. Copyright expired).*
Figure 76: **Layout of the House of Trebius Valens.**
Figure 77: **Photograph of the Armaturarum (before its collapse).**
Figure 78: **Interior of the Armaturarum from a postcard by Edizione Domenico Trampetti** *(c/o Wikimedia Commons. Copyright expired.)*
Figure 79: **The Garden of the House of Octavius Quartius.** *Picture Credit: Magister Mercator/Wikimedia Commons.*
Figure 80: **Layout of the House of Octavius Quartius**
Figure 81: **Fresco of Venus in a shell, garden of the House of the Marine Venus.**
Figure 82: **Layout of the House of the Marine Venus.**
Figure 83: **Fresco of Garden Features, garden of the House of the Marine Venus.**
Figure 84: **Still Life with Eggs, Birds and Bronze dishes from the House of Julia Felix. National Museum of Naples.** *Public domain, Wikimedia Commons*
Figure 85: **Layout of the Properties of Julia Felix**
Figure 86: **Photograph of a Pompeiian Vineyard.**

PICTURE CREDITS

Figure 87: **Mosaic of Vineyard workers**. *Google Images. Public Domain*
Figure 88: **Photograph of the Amphitheatre.**
Figure 89: **Photograph of dedicatory inscription.**
Figure 90: **Graffiti of a fight between Marcus Attilius and Felix.** *Google Images. Public Domain*
Figure 91: **Fresco of the Riot at the amphitheatre**. *UDF Paris (c/o Wikimedia Commons. Released into Public Domain.)*
Fig 92: **Vesuvius and Pompeii**. *Picture Credit: Robert S Duncanson. Public Domain. Wikimedia Commons.*
Figure 93: **Pompeii's Last Days Tour Route.**
Figure 94: **Fresco of fruit from the Villa Oplontis**. *Public Domain Image. Google Images*
Figure 95: **Body cast with heavy clothing**. *Picture Credit: Carlo Mirante Creative Commons 2.0 Generic Licence.*
Figure 96: **The Forum**
Fig 97: **Fresco of Vesuvius, pre 79AD.** *Public domain c/o Wikimedia*
Fig 98: **The Entrance of the Macellum with view of money-lender booths.**
Fig 99: **Fresco of forum scene from the House of Julia Felix.** *Public domain c/o Wikimedia commons.*
Fig 100: **Photo of Modestus's bakery.**
Fig 101: **Vesuvius and the eruption column.** *Public domain on Wikimedia commons c/o the Discovery channel and creative crew.*
Fig 102: **photo of the junction between the Via dell Abbondanza and the Via Stabiana.**
Fig 103: **Volcanic rock from Vesuvius** *c/o Rob Lavinsky. Creative Commons share alike license 3.0 on Wikimedia commons.*
Fig 104: **Statue of the Ephebe.** *c/o Sailko (Wikimedia commons). GNU Free Licence.*
Figure 105: **Layout of the House of Ephebe**
Fig 106: **Fresco of Menander from the House of Menander.** *Public domain c/o Wikimedia commons.*

PICTURE CREDITS

Figure 107: **Lanterns.** *Photograph by Giorgio Somer. Public Domain c/o Wikimedia commons.*
Fig 108: **Layout of the House of Menander**
Fig 109: **Karl Briullov-The Last Day of Pompeii.** *Public Domain c/o Wikimedia commons.*
Figure 110: **Layout of the House of Queen Caroline.**
Fig 111: **Photo of Vesuvius from southern end of forum.**
Fig 112: **William Marlow: Vesuvius erupting by night.** *Public domain. Wikimedia commons.*
Figure 113: **Fresco from the House of the Golden Bracelet.** *Picture Credit: Stefano Bolognini.*
Fig 114. **Fresco from Garden Room, House of the Golden Bracelet** *Picture Credit: Stefano Bolognini.*
Figure 115: **Cast of a child from the House of the Golden Bracelet.** *Picture Credit: Fer.Filol, Public Domain, c/o Wikimedia Commons.*
Fig 116: **Photo of the Herculaneum Gate from the street of tombs.**
Figure 117: **The Street of Tombs**
Fig 118: **Computer animation of pyroclastic surge. Original source: US government.** *Public Domain c/o Wikimedia commons.*
Fig 119: **Frieze of the Dionysian Mysteries, The Villa of the Mysteries.** *Picture Credit: Ancient Goths, Public Domain Image. c/o Wikimedia Commons*
Figure 120: **Layout of the Villa of the Mysteries.**
Fig 121: **Photo of the entrance to the Villa Diomedes.**
Fig 122: **Layout of the Villa Diomedes**
Figure 123: **Death and the wheels of fortune.** *Creative commons attribution 2.0m generic c/o Wikimedia commons.*
Fig 124: **Mosaic from the entrance to the House of Orpheus.** *Public Domain. Google Images*
Fig 125: **Cast of dog from the house of Orpheus.** *Photo by Claus Ableiter. GNU Free Document License c/o Wikimedia commons.*
Figure 126: **Layout of the House of Orpheus.**

PICTURE CREDITS

Fig 127: **Skeletons.** *Public Domain Image c/o Wikimedia Commons and Discover Channel and Creative Crew.*

Figure 128: **Reconstruction of the House of the Painters at Work in the Boboli Gardens, Florence**. *Public Domain. Wikimedia Commons*

Figure 129: **Carpe Diem.** *Photo by Marie Lan Nguyen. Public domain c/o Wikimedia commons.*

Fig 130: **Photo of large palestra**

Fig 131: **Layout of the palestra**.

Fig 132: **Caste of victim found at large palestra**. *Photo by Ken Thomas. Public domain c/o Wikimedia commons.*

Fig 133: **Bodies in the garden of the Fugitives**. *Photo by Lance Vortex. Creative commons attribution Share alike 3.0 c/o Wikimedia commons.*

Fig 134: **The final fugitive.** *Photo by Daniele Florio. Creative commons attribution Share alike 3.0 c/o Wikimedia commons.*

Figure 135: **Vesuvius from the Ruins of Pompeii**

Fig 136: **Diagram showing how ash preserved the body shape of the victims.** *Picture Credit:* fer. Filol. Public Domain c/o Wikimedia commons.

Fig 137: **Victims found at the Nuceria gate**. *Photo by fer. Filol. Public domain c/o Wikimedia commons.*

BIBLIOGRAPHY

Ancient Texts

The Institutes of Gaius
Isidore of Seville, *Etymologies.*
Marcus Aurelius, *Meditations*
Pliny the Elder, *Natural History.*
Pliny the Younger, *Letters*
Strabo, *Geography.*
Seneca, *Epistles*
Seneca, *Natural Questions*
Varro, *On Agriculture.*
Vitruvius, *The Ten Books of Architecture.*

Articles

Ball, Larry, F and Dobbins, J (2013) *"Pompeii Forum Project: Current Thinking on the Pompeii Forum"* **American Journal of Archaeology.**

De Caro, S *"Nuove indagini sulle fortificazioni di Pompeii* "**AION** , 1985, vol 7

Mastrolorenzo, G, Petrone, PP, Papplardo, L, Guavino, FM et al (2010) *"Lethal Thermal Impact at Periphery of Pyroclastic Surges: Evidences at Pompeii."* **PLOS One.**

Petrone, PP, (2011). *"Human Corpses as time Capsules: New perspectives in the Study of Past Man's Disasters."* **Journal of Anthropological Sciences 89:1-4.**

Rolandi, G, (2008) *" The 79AD eruption of Somma: The Relationship between the date of the eruption and the southeast tephra dispersion."* **Science Direct.**

Sheldon, N. *"Dating the Eruption of Vesuvius that destroyed Pompeii",* **History and Archaeology Online.**

Sheldon, N, *"Suffocation Versus Thermal Shock: How did the people of Pompeii die?".* **History and Archaeology Online,**

Sigurdsson, H, (1985), *"The Eruption of Vesuvius in AD 79".* **NatGeogRes, Vol 1.3.**

Stefani, Grete, (2006). *"The Actual Date of the Eruption."* **Archeo n.10 p260.**

Books

Beard, Mary, (2009). *Pompeii: The Life of a Roman Town*. Profile Books.

Clarke, G, (2016) *Pompeii*. Palala Press.

Conticello, B, (1989) *Pompeii Archaeological Guide*.

Cooley, A E and M G L, (2004). *Pompeii: A Sourcebook*. Routledge: London and New York

D'Ambra (1993) *Roman Art in Context: An anthology*.

Deem, James M (2005). *Bodies from the Ash: Life and Death in Ancient Pompeii*. Houghton Mifflin Company.

Dobbins, J J and Foss, P W (eds) (2008) The World of Pompeii. Routledge: London and New York.

Faas, P, (2003) *Around the Roman Table*.

Grant, Michael, (2005). *Cities of Vesuvius: Pompeii and Herculaneum.* Folio Society.
Lazer, Estelle (2011). *Resurrecting Pompeii.* Routledge.
Meijer, F, *The Gladiators: History's Most Dangerous Sport*
Richardson, L, *Pompeii: An Architectural History.*
Roberts, Paul (2013) *Life and Death in Pompeii and Herculaneum.* The British Museum.
Sigurdsson, H, (1999) *Melting the Earth: The History of Ideas on Volcanic Eruptions.* New York: Oxford University Press.
Wallace-Hadrill, A, (1994) *Houses and Society in Pompeii and Herculaneum.* Princetown.
Wilkinson, P (2003) *Pompeii: The Last Day.* BBC Books.
Zanker, P, (2000). *Pompeii: Public and Private Life.* Harvard.

Websites
79 AD: https://sites.google.com/site/ad79eruption/
The Pompeii Forum Project: Pompeii.virginia.edu
Pompeii: The Mystery of the People Frozen in Time, BBC Two.

FOOTNOTES

1. Civic Pompeii

Early Pompeii

1 De Caro, *Nuore Indagini* P101-3
2 De Caro, *Tempio di Apollo*
3 De Caro, *Nuore Indagini*
4 *The World of Pompeii*, P12
5 *Geography*, IV.4-8
6 *Natural History III* 60-62

A Crossroad of Cultures

1 *Dictionary.com*
2 Isidore, *Etymologies XV.1.51*

Hellenisation

1 *Ten Books of Architecture, Book V, Ch 6*
2 Strabo, *Geography, 14.1*

FOOTNOTES

3 *Cooley and Cooley, A9, p9*

Introduction to the Forum

1 *The world of Pompeii, p133*

Governing Pompeii

1 *The World of Pompeii,* P11
2 *Cooley and Cooley,* P77

The Roman Conquest

1 Conticello, p49

Cultural Change

1 Cooley and Cooley, P20

New Civic Amenities

1 *Mediations, 8.24*
2 *The Ten Books of Architecture V.10.2*
3 *The Ten Books of Architecture V.10.1*

Slaves and Civic Religion

1 Varro *On Agriculture I.17*
2 *Institutes of Gaius, 53*

The Augustan Forum

1. *The World of Pompeii p161*

The Imperial Cult

1 Pompeii Forum Project, p461-492

Women in Pompeii

1. Richardson, p198

The Rise of the Mystery Cult

1 *The World of Pompeii, p79*
2 Cooley and Cooley, P110

2 Discovering Pompeii

Public Bathing

1 Seneca, *letters to Lucius, 56*

The State of the Streets

1 *The World of Pompeii, P264*
2 *Beard*

Popular Religion

1 Cooley and Cooley, P109

Innovative Housing

1. Vitruvius, *The ten Books of Architecture, VI.II.I*

Interior Design

FOOTNOTES

1 Cooley and Cooley, P123

Ordinary Apartments

1. Beard, Ch 3

A High Class leisure Centre

1. Cooley and Cooley, P171

Vintage Pompeii

1. *Natural History, XIX.70*

2. Pompeii's Last Days

Introduction

1 Pliny the Younger, *Letters BK 6.16*
2 Interview with the Author: *"Dating the Eruption of Vesuvius that destroyed Pompeii"*, **History and Archaeology Online.**
3 Stefani, 2006
4 Interview with the Author: *"Dating the Eruption of Vesuvius that destroyed Pompeii"*, **History and Archaeology Online.**

Signs and Portents

1 Seneca, *Natural Questions, BK 6*
2 Pliny the Younger, *Letters, 6.20*

Vesuvius Awakes

1. Pliny the Younger, *Letters, 6.16*

The Umberella Pine

1 Sigurdsson, et al *P39-51*
2 *Letters 6.16*

A Lethal Rainfall

1 *Letters 6.16*

Hiding Treasure

1 Sigurdsson et al P39-51

The Violence Escalates

1 Sigurdsson et al, P39-51

No Refuge

Letters, 6.21

Midnight terrors

1 Sigurdsson et al P39-51
2 *Letters Book 6*
3 Sigurdsson et al P39-51

The Early Hours of the Morning

1 *Letters 6.16*

The Third Surge Part 1

1 Pliny the Younger, *letters 6.16*

FOOTNOTES

2. Mastrolorenzo, G et al

The Fourth Surge

1 Sigurdsson et al, P39-51
2 Cooley and Cooley, P121

The End of Pompeii

1-5 Interview with the author, *Suffocation Versus Thermal Shock: How did the people of Pompeii die?* **History and Archaeology Online,**
6 Pliny the Younger, *Letters 6.21*
7 Pliny the Younger, *Letters 6.21*
8 Pliny the Younger, *Letters 6.21*

ABOUT THE AUTHOR

Natasha Sheldon studied Ancient History and Archaeology at Leicester and Bristol Universities in the UK. She was awarded the Arnold Wycombe Gomme prize for Ancient History and holds a BA Honours in Ancient History and Archaeology and a MA in Ancient History and Historiography.

Natasha researches and writes mainly on the subjects of history and archaeology, however her specialist area is Roman history. Both of her dissertations in the field of magic and religion in the Roman Empire have been published. They are: The Origins and Meaning of Roman Witchcraft and Roman Magic and Religion in Late Antiquity. Natasha is currently involved in further research in this area.

Natasha has travelled widely across Europe and the Middle East and has first-hand experience of many ancient sites - Roman and otherwise. A few examples of sites she has explored are Pompeii, Herculaneum, Rome in Italy, Leptis Magna in Libya, Jerash in Jordan and Palmyra in Syria. There are many others!

Many of her journeys have been motivated by her studies but also by her love of exploration-at home and abroad. She loves to experience other cultures. Adventures to date include riding camels in the Sahara, visiting Tripoli and having tea with the Bedouin.

Natasha's articles have been published by Italianvisits.com and Travel Thru history, Decoded Science, Decoded Past and History Collection. Her website Historyandarchaeologyonline.com is a growing resource for anyone studying or interested in history and archaeology.

facebook.com/NatashaSheldonAuthor
twitter.com/Hypatia2

ALSO BY NATASHA SHELDON

Not a Guide to Leicester

Leicester in 100 Dates

The Little Book of Leicestershire

Printed in Great Britain
by Amazon